THE KNITTER'S BIBLE
baby knits

LAURA LONG

David and Charles
www.rucraft.co.uk

A DAVID & CHARLES BOOK
Copyright © David & Charles Limited 2010

David & Charles is an F+W Media Inc. company
4700 East Galbraith Road
Cincinnati, OH 45236

First published in the UK and US in 2010

Text and designs copyright © Laura Long 2010
Photography, illustrations and layout copyright © David & Charles 2010

ISBN-13: 978-0-7153-3766-0 paperback
ISBN-10: 0-7153-3766-1 paperback

Printed in China by RR Donnelley
for David & Charles
Brunel House, Newton Abbot, Devon

Publisher: Alison Myer
Acquisitions Editor: Jennifer Fox-Proverbs
Editor: James Brooks
Project Editor: Lorraine Slipper
Proofreader: Bethany Dymond
Design Manager: Sarah Clark
Photographer: Lorna Yabsley and Sam Atkinson
Production Controller: Kelly Smith

David & Charles publish high quality books on a wide range of subjects.
For more great book ideas visit: **www.rucraft.co.uk**

DB

THE KNITTER'S BIBI

baby |

contents

introduction

When I started writing this book I asked all my friends with children, babies, nieces and nephews for ideas about ideal projects to include. I wanted to create a book full of adorable projects that people would want to knit and that they wouldn't be able to find anywhere else; projects that they could be creative with and that would make use of all the beautiful yarns available in the shops.

Here you will find a range of garments, toys and accessories for every baby and every occasion. There are gorgeous outfits for newborn babies that would make the perfect christening gifts, practical clothes for baby to play in, cuddly toys for baby to play with, soft and snuggly accessories to wrap up warm in, and even the cutest pyjama bag for storing your baby's favourite sleepsuit.

Whether you are a complete beginner or a knitting pro, you will find a project suitable for you. Simple mittens and hats are ideal projects to start with, while the more complicated knit structures on the pinafore dress and cardigans are perfect for the more experienced knitter.

For each project I have suggested alternative yarns and colourways to make the designs as unique as the baby you are knitting for. You will be amazed at how different the final appearance can be, simply by substituting the yarns used. You can make a beautiful garment for a girl by knitting in pretty pinks, then make the same garment look masculine by knitting with a range of blues. Or try knitting a piece in woollen rustic colours for winter and then transforming it with light cotton yarns for summer. The only limit is your imagination!

Yarn Focus explains why I have chosen a particular yarn, while Design Secrets Unravelled… suggests alternative yarns and colourways to use to completely change the appearance of the design. Many of the projects blend several yarns together to create a new more exciting yarn to knit with. This enables you to be a lot more creative and make the piece completely unique to you.

Embellishment also plays an important part in transforming a design and you can have fun altering the colour, size or style of the buttons or adding embroidery, such as the little animals on the cuffs of the mittens. Each stitch you make will transform the piece and make it something for your baby to treasure.

The beauty about hand knitting something, especially a gift for a new born baby, is that it never gets thrown away. A handmade gift is cherished forever and passed down and enjoyed for years to come… even if it eventually ends up being used to dress up a toy! Another joy about knitting for babies is that due to the size of the garments, they are usually quick to knit, giving you more time on your hands to enjoy your little one.

Knitting should be fun and enable you to let your creativity flow. By experimenting with different yarns and colours, you can really see what knitting has to offer, and knitting something for a baby to love will also make you the envy of all your friends!

Happy knitting! x

in the beginning . . .

fibres

When choosing yarns for a project it is important to consider how the finished item will be used. Most baby items will get a lot of wear and tear, so hard-wearing yarns made from wool, cotton or soft synthetics are most suitable – and many of them are machine-washable, which may be important for a busy mother. But you can still use more delicate yarns – why not use silky or sparkly yarn in the borders of the Peekaboo Pocket Cardigan (page 62) or the bodice of the Pretty Pinafore Dress (page 56) and make your child something special to wear to parties.

NATURAL FIBRES

Natural fibres come from both animals and plants. They may cost more than synthetic fibres, but many people prefer the feel of them. They tend to take dyes better than synthetic fibres, so you may find a better range of colours in yarns made from natural fibres. On the other hand, natural fibres often require more careful handling and cleaning, so you may think it better to use synthetic yarn for items that will get a lot of wear and will need to be washed often, such as baby clothes.

Alpaca yarns have become widely available in recent years. As a member of the camel family, alpacas are raised for their fleece as they are too small to be used as pack animals, as is their relative the llama. Two qualities of alpaca yarn are available: yarn from the Huacaya which produces a dense, soft fleece with a crimped effect and yarn from the Suri, whose longer mop-like fleece is considered superior. Alpaca fleece is similar to sheep's wool, but is lighter, silkier, warmer and has less lanolin. It is also similar to cashmere, but much less expensive!

Angora yarn is made from fibres from the coat of the angora rabbit. It is soft and silky with a fluffy haze that makes items that are very soft and warm. Angora fibre is usually mixed with other fibres as it has little natural elasticity. Items made from angora yarns require special care but are well worth the effort.

Cashmere yarns are the epitome of luxury. They are made from the undercoat of the Kashmir goat, and harvested by combing it off the animal rather than shearing. Cashmere fibres are fine and soft, yet strong and can be made into a very warm fabric. Pure cashmere yarns are very expensive; the more affordable versions mix cashmere with other fibres, such as wool.

Cotton fibres are collected from the seed case of the cotton bush and are then spun tightly to produce a yarn. Mercerized cotton yarns undergo a process of pre-shrinking which also leaves them with a glossy sheen. Yarns that blend cotton with other fibres are common, since this not only makes the cotton yarn lighter, but it also compensates for cotton's lack of elasticity. Pure cotton yarns are ideal for showing off textured stitch patterns, as the stitches will lie flatter than those made in wool. Use cotton yarns to produce items that are both hard-wearing and comfortable to wear in warmer weather.

Linen fibres are manufactured from the stem of the flax plant. This fibre has little elasticity and can have a stiff, crunchy feel. You will often find it in a blend with cotton, which produces a softer fibre, but many people prefer the drape of a pure linen fabric.

Mohair fibres are long and quite weak, so they are often blended with other fibres for strength. The yarn made from mohair fibres is very light and warm with a high lustre and sheen. This fibre comes from the coat of the angora goat; fibres from the coats of goats up to 18 months old are called kid mohair.

Silk yarn has a smooth, soft texture. It is made from the cocoon of the silkworm, which is spun into a yarn. Silk is one of the strongest natural fibres and is comfortable to wear all year round.

Wool is usually understood to refer to the sheep of a fleece. Wool yarn has natural elasticity and is easy to work. It can be unravelled and reused if desired. It is an all-year-round fibre, offering both good insulation and absorption. There are different qualities of wool depending on the breed of sheep that supplied it. Merino wool, from merino sheep which live in milder climates, is finer and softer than, say, Shetland wool from sheep which live in colder climates. Lambswool is yarn produced from the first shearing of an animal and is usually the softest yarn that an animal will produce.

BLENDED AND SYNTHETIC FIBRES

The most common synthetic fibres are polyester, acrylic and polypropylene. These are made by adding chemicals to non-fibrous substances. They have the advantage of being hard-wearing and machine-washable. Synthetic fibres are used for novelty yarns such as ribbon and eyelash yarns. They can also be mixed with natural fibres to reduce cost and increase elasticity. Many excellent synthetic and synthetic/natural fibre mix yarns are produced today especially for making clothes and toys for babies and children.

FIBRE CHECKLIST

When you are choosing yarn for a knitted project for a baby, use the checklist below to see what qualities your yarn offers.

Hard-wearing: Blended and synthetic fibres, cotton, linen, wool
Luxury: Cashmere, silk
Soft and snuggly: Alpaca, angora, mohair

weight

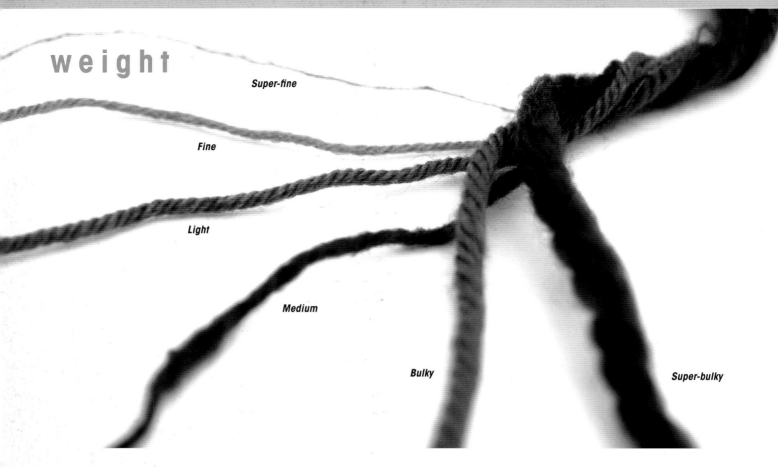

Super-fine

Fine

Light

Medium

Bulky

Super-bulky

Yarns are classified by their thickness; we refer to this as the weight of the yarn. The weight of a yarn you use can have a big impact on the way your knitting looks. Patterns will look very different when they are knitted in a fine, light-weight yarn that will produce a delicate fabric, than if they are knitted in a medium-weight or bulky yarn that will produce a much thicker fabric. One of the joys of knitting is to experiment with the different weights of yarn to see what effects you can achieve.

PLY OR THICKNESS

Plying is the process used to create a strong and balanced yarn. Plied yarn is made from strands of yarn – known as singles – that are twisted together. The most common combinations are two, three or four ply. You should not assume that the more plies there are, the thicker the yarn is, since much depends on the size of the original fibre and the spinning process used to produce the yarn: a yarn that is tightly spun will be thinner than one that is loosely spun. For instance, a 2ply Shetland wool will knit as a fine weight (4ply) yarn while the traditional thick Icelandic Lopi wool is formed of only a single ply.

The yarn requirements in this book refer to the standard names developed by the Craft Yarn Council of America, which divides yarns into weights rather than numbers of plies. This is to avoid the confusion that can arise between the different terms used by US and UK yarn manufacturers for the same weights of yarn. In each of the projects UK yarn equivalents are given in brackets, and the chart of standard yarn weights on this page should enable to you to find a suitable yarn for any project in this book wherever in the world you do your knitting.

STANDARD YARN WEIGHTS

weight	gauge*	needle size**	yarn type***
super-fine	27–32 sts	1 to 3 (2.25–3.25mm)	sock, fingering (2ply, 3ply)
fine	23–26 sts	3 to 5 (3.25–3.75mm)	sport, baby (4ply)
light	21–24 sts	5 to 7 (3.75–4.5mm)	light worsted, DK (DK)
medium	16–20 sts	7 to 9 (4.5–5.5mm)	worsted, afghan (aran)
bulky	12–15 sts	9 to 11 (5.5–8mm)	chunky
super-bulky	6–11 sts	11 (8mm) and above	super-chunky

Notes: * Gauge (tension) is measured over 4in/10cm in stockinette (stocking) stitch
** US needle sizes are given first, with UK equivalents in brackets
*** Alternative US yarn type names are given first, with UK equivalents in brackets

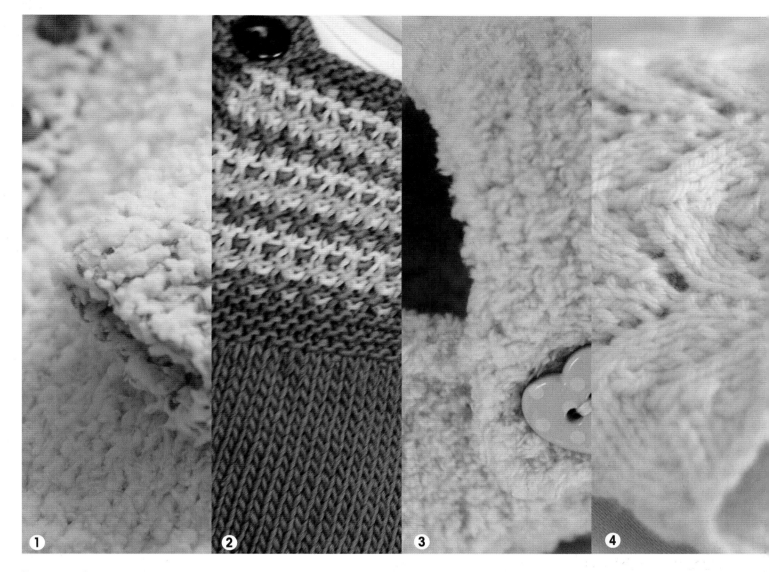

1 2 3 4

texture

Yarns are available in a whole variety of different textures, from thin, smooth and soft, to fuzzy and thick. The yarns you choose can dramatically change the appearance of a piece. Try knitting the same garment, accessory or toy in different textured yarns and colours. You will be amazed at the transformation between each piece.

COMBINING YARNS (1)

Many projects combine together several yarns to create one single knitting yarn. You can be really creative with the yarns you combine and produce a piece of work that is completely unique. Try mixing a fine, brightly coloured yarn with a thick fluffy yarn: little flecks of colour flash though the fluffy yarn creating a really interesting effect (see Cosy Toes Warmer, page 78). Or try blending three or four different coloured yarns all of the same texture and thickness: a tweed appearance is created in a random way (see Simple Hooded Cardigan, page 50). Using a cotton yarn next to a woollen or cashmere mix yarn gives a completely different drape to the fabric (see So Stripy Sweater, page 44).

CREATING PATTERNS (2)

When knitting a complex knit structure, it is best to use a smoother yarn without too much texture so that all your hard work creating the stitches is not lost. In this situation you can be more experimental with your choice of colour (see Pinafore Dress, page 56) and choose colours to really enhance the pattern.

EXPERIMENTING WITH YARN (3)

Be experimental with the yarn but try to stick to yarns that need needles of the same thickness to those I have suggested. This is especially so when knitting clothes and shoes (see Bootee Cuties, page 20), as the size of the completed garment can change dramatically using different sized needles. However, for toys (see Happy Bunny, page 70, and Cute Chicken Mobile, page 84) and accessories (see Funky Floral Pyjama Bag, page 96,) you can really let your imagination run wild with your choice of yarns and you can alter the needle sizes as you don't have to worry too much about the size of the finished piece.

USING SOFT YARNS (4)

A baby's skin is delicate so it is very important that the yarn you choose should feel soft and huggable against it (see Beautiful Blanket, page 90). All my yarn suggestions pay great importance to this.

colour

The colours you choose can really change the appearance of a piece. Spend time selecting the right colour combinations whether it is for a boy or a girl, or if you are making clothes for spring, summer, autumn or winter. The colours you choose can really transform the garment as well as highlighting the stitches.

COLOURS FOR SEASONS

Spring – light pale colours are ideal for spring days. Think of daffodils and blossom and picnics in the garden. Pastel shades such as pink, mint green, and lilac combined with neutral whites and creams make the perfect spring piece, (see Pretty Pinafore Dress, page 56).

Summer – bright fresh colours such as yellow, blue, pink and green are great for summer. Think of beach balls and summer holidays. Add flashes of a brightly coloured yarn to more muted colours to take you from spring to summer, (see Funky Floral Pyjama Bag, page 96).

Autumn – use rustic colours such as mossy greens, browns and reds, using the changing colours of leaves for inspiration. Combine several shades together in one yarn for a random tweed appearance, (see Cosy Toes Warmer, page 78).

Winter – this is the perfect season to bring out red shades. Combine a bright red with dark colours for that burst of Christmas cheer or use red with green to echo holly, (see Animal Mittens, page 24).

FEMININE COLOURS (1)

Pinks and pastel colours are often associated with girls. Try combining different shades of pink together for a really feminine appearance. You could even add a pink yarn to more neutral colours to give that subtle feminine edge, (see Pretty in Pink, page 48).

MASCULINE COLOURS (2)

Blues and brighter colours tend to be associated with boys. There are so many different shades of blue, ranging from pale powder blue to a deep navy, (see So Stripy Sweater, page 44).

NEUTRAL COLOURS (3)

If you don't know whether a baby is going to be a boy or a girl, you could choose a neutral shade such as white or cream and accentuate this with a bright button or ribbon once the baby is born, (see Lovely Lacy Set, page 30).

BRIGHT COLOURS (4)

If you want your baby to stand out from the crowd, dress them in striking reds, yellows and blues. Bold colours can really accentuate their features and look particularly great on boys, (see Bobbles and Stripes set, page 38).

PASTEL COLOURS (5)

Soft pinks, baby blues, light greens, lilacs and creams are the favoured colours for young babies and it is easy to see why, (see Simple Hooded Cardigan, page 50).

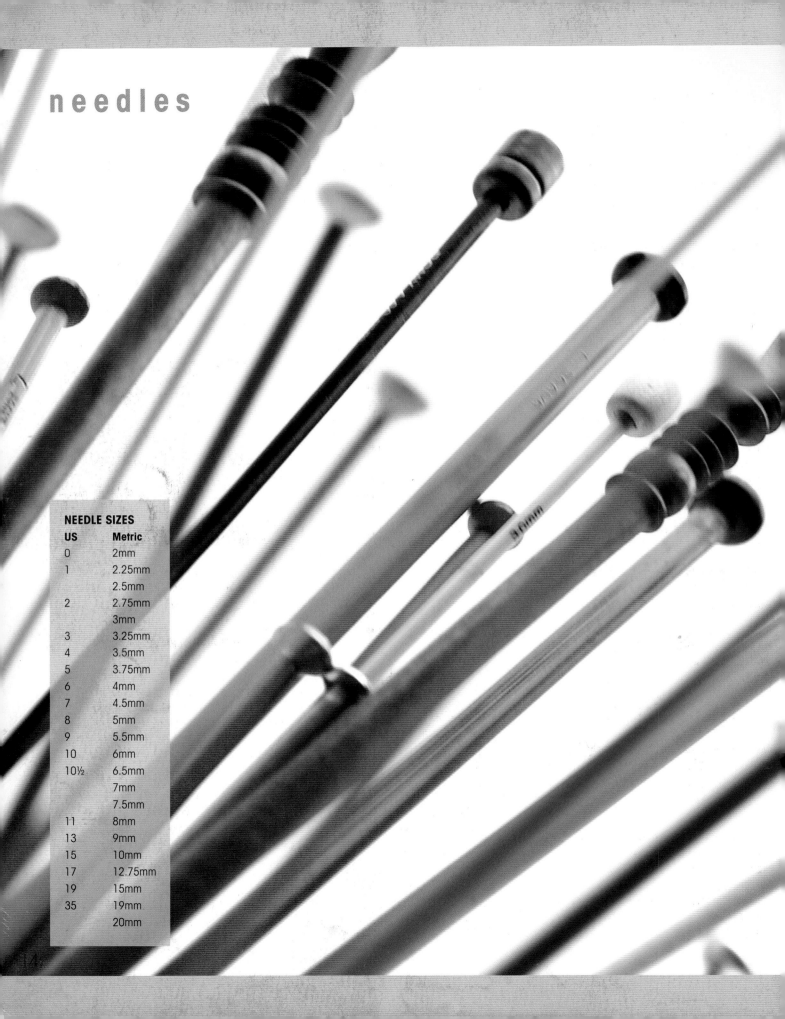

needles

NEEDLE SIZES

US	Metric
0	2mm
1	2.25mm
	2.5mm
2	2.75mm
	3mm
3	3.25mm
4	3.5mm
5	3.75mm
6	4mm
7	4.5mm
8	5mm
9	5.5mm
10	6mm
10½	6.5mm
	7mm
	7.5mm
11	8mm
13	9mm
15	10mm
17	12.75mm
19	15mm
35	19mm
	20mm

gauge

The gauge (tension) of a knitted fabric depends on the stitch pattern used, the weight of the yarn, the size of knitting needles and the tension that the individual knitter puts on the yarn as it passes through his or her fingers. It is important to keep an even tension on the yarn to produce an even fabric. All patterns will state the number of stitches and rows needed to make a 4in (10cm) sample of fabric. Please take time to check your gauge before starting your project to make sure that your finished item is the correct size.

GAUGE (TENSION) MEASUREMENT

The best way to check your gauge is to knit a square of fabric measuring at least 6in (15cm) with the yarn, needles and stitch(es) you will use for the project. Making a larger square than necessary allows for accurate measurement in the middle of the fabric, avoiding any edges that may have distorted.

Quite often you will not be able to get both the exact stitch and row count that you need. The stitch count is usually the most important, as this will affect the width of your item; if the stitch count is not right, your item could be too wide or too narrow. It is easier to adjust the row count by knitting fewer or more rows where necessary to get the right length. But be aware of patterns that give instructions to decrease or increase over an exact number of rows – you may need to recalculate these to make sure your item is the right length.

KNITTING A GAUGE (TENSION) SQUARE

Gauge squares are usually knitted in stockinette (stocking) stitch.

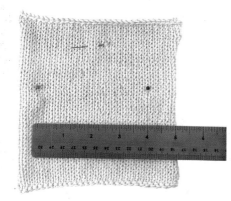

1 Cast on the number of stitches given to measure 4in (10cm) plus half as many again.
2 Work 6in (15cm) in stockinette stitch and bind off loosely.
3 Use the same method you will use to press the finished item to press your gauge square (see page 119).

4 Lay your fabric on a flat surface without stretching it. Use a ruler to measure 1in (2.5cm) in from one edge and mark with a pin.
5 Measure 4in (10cm) from the first pin and mark with another pin.
6 Avoiding the cast-on and bound-off edges which may distort the fabric, mark the same measurements vertically.
7 Work out your gauge by counting the number of stitches and rows between the pins. If there are more than the pattern states, the square is too small: make another square with a needle a size larger. If there are fewer stitches than stated in the pattern, the square is too big: make another square using a needle a size smaller.
8 Measure and reknit your gauge squares in the same way until you get the gauge for the pattern.

MEASURING TEXTURED YARN

It can be difficult to see the stitches in yarn with a rough texture or long pile. Try holding a long-pile fabric up to the light to make this easier, making sure to protect your eyes from strong light. Mark the stitches with long ends of yarn in a contrasting colour rather than pins. When making a gauge

square in highly textured yarn such as bouclé or chenille, try knitting a strand of sewing cotton in a contrasting cotton; this will help the stitches to show up. Use yarn ends in a contrasting colour rather than pins to mark your measurements. This avoids the pins falling out if you need to stretch out the fabric slightly to see the stitches. It might be

easier to see the stitches on the reverse side of the fabric for some yarns – this is particularly the case for gauge squares worked in stockinette stitch.

MEASURING OVER A STITCH PATTERN

If you are instructed to work the gauge square over a stitch pattern other than stockinette stitch, you need to work on enough stitches to be able to complete repeats of the pattern. Pattern repeats are usually the stitches given in a row after an asterisk, which are then repeated until the end of the row. Cast on a multiple of this number of stitches together with any extra stitches worked at the beginning and the end of a row.

USING GAUGE (TENSION) FOR SUBSTITUTING YARNS

You are free to choose any yarn you like to make the projects in this book. If you do substitute a yarn, it is very important to check your gauge in the new yarn so that your items are the right size. Instructions for working out how much yarn you will need are on page 124.

abbreviations

All knitting patterns abbreviate instructions for the sake of brevity. The following is a list of all the abbreviations you need to make the projects in this book.

alt	alternate
approx	approximately
beg	begin/beginning
cm	centimetre(s)
cont	continue
dec(s)	decrease(s)/decreasing
DK	double knitting
foll	following
g	gram
g st	garter stitch (k every row)
in(s)	inch(es)
inc(s)	increase(s)/increasing
k	knit
k2tog	knit 2 stitches together (decrease 1 stitch)
k3tog	knit 3 stitches together (decrease 2 stitches)
LH	left hand
m	metre(s)
mm	millimetre(s)
M1	make one (increase 1 stitch)
MB	make a bobble
oz	ounces
p	purl
patt(s)	pattern(s)
patt rep(s)	pattern repeat(s)
p2tog	purl 2 stitches together (decrease 1 stitch)
p3tog	purl 3 stitches together (decrease 2 stitches)
psso	pass slipped stitch over
rem	remain/ing

rep(s)	repeat(s)
rev st st	reverse stockinette stitch (1 row p, 1 row k)
RH	right hand
RS	right side
skpo	slip 1 stitch, knit 1 stitch, pass slipped stitch over (1 stitch decreased)
sl 1	slip 1 stitch
ssk	slip 2 stitches one at a time, knit 2 slipped stitches together (decrease 1 stitch)
ssp	slip 2 stitches one at a time, purl 2 slipped stitches together through the back of the loops (decrease 1 stitch)
st(s)	stitch(es)
st st	stockinette stitch (1 row k, 1 row p) (UK: stocking stitch)
tog	together
WS	wrong side
wyib	with yarn in back
wyif	with yarn in front
ybwd	yarn backward
yd(s)	yard(s)
yfwd	yarn forward
yo	yarn over
*	repeat directions following * as many times as indicated or until end of row
( )	repeat instructions in round brackets the number of times stated

In the instructions for the projects, I have favoured US knitting terms. Refer to this box for the UK equivalent.

US TERM	UK TERM
bind off	cast off
gauge	tension
stockinette stitch	stocking stitch
reverse stockinette stitch	reverse stocking stitch
seed stitch	moss stitch
moss stitch	double moss stitch

reading knitting patterns

Knitting patterns are a set of instructions that tell you how to knit and sew up an item. They use lots of abbreviations and shorthand phrases to save space and avoid unnecessary repetition of instructions. New knitters may find this quite daunting, but a list of abbreviation definitions is always given – those for this book are on page 16. Knitters soon become familiar with commonly used abbreviations such as k and p. If there are any unfamiliar abbreviations, make sure that you read the definitions carefully before you start knitting.

WORKING FROM CHARTS

Written instructions for charted patterns are usually quite sparse – they will tell you how many stitches to cast on and bind off and possibly how to incorporate shaping into the item. Sometimes instructions for shaping and for working the different sizes in a pattern with multiple sizes will be shown on the chart itself. Working from charts is explained along with the technique for intarsia on page 112 and instructions for working a pattern in Fair Isle can be found on page 114.

IMPERIAL AND METRIC MEASUREMENTS

Both imperial (inches and ounces) and metric (centimetres and grams) measurements are given for all patterns in this book. You should make sure you stick to one set of measurements when making a project; most of the conversions are exact, but there are some that have been approximated because of problems with conversion from one system to another. If you mix the two systems, you may end up with an item that does not fit.

COMMON SHORTHAND PHRASES

cont as set Continue to work as instructed by the pattern.

keeping patt correct Work the pattern as instructed, while carrying out a new instruction. For instance, keeping patt correct, dec 1 st at each end of next row.

work as given for Where you make more than one piece that is similar to another, for instance sleeves or a left and right mitten, follow the instructions for the first piece to a certain point, which is usually marked by asterisks.

* Repeat any instructions after an asterisk to the end of a row or as many times as the pattern states.

** Double asterisks usually mark the beginning and/or end of a set of instructions which will be repeated.

( ) Any instructions in round brackets should be repeated the number of times indicated.

The Funky Floral Pyjama Bag (see pages 96–99) has a bold, modern pattern that is worked from the colour chart provided.

and now
to knit…

bootee cuties

These sweet little shoes not only help to keep your baby's feet warm but they also make a colourful statement. By making simple changes to the basic pattern, such as using different stripe combinations and stitch techniques and varying your yarn choice, you can easily create an array of different shoes to complement your baby's favourite outfits. All the shoes have a little strap clasped with buttons in a variety of styles and colours for a cute and practical finishing touch. You could even try and recreate your own 'real' knitted shoes to match your baby's!

These strap bootees are a stylish and practical alternative to traditional bootees.

YARN FOCUS

You could knit these shoes using any yarn, but you need to remember that the thicker the yarn and bigger the needle, the bigger the shoe will be. This is evident in the blue fluffy shoe, which has been knitted in a thick yarn to keep little toes warm. All the yarns I have used are soft and comfortable even without a sock underneath. Your yarn choice and colour combination would be dictated by the child's outfit or the time of year.

DESIGN SECRETS UNRAVELLED...

The shoes are suitable for both babies and toddlers. They could be used as slippers or knitted to match an outfit. I wanted to make them look more grown up than booties, so added a strap to imitate a real shoe. The strap also allows you to select interesting buttons as a fastening to make each pair unique.

The shoes have been knitted in a variety of colours and stitches. The basic shoe pattern uses stockinette stitch and relies on the yarn to add texture. The pink shoe uses seed stitch to give a textured knit structure. The striped shoes enable you to mix and experiment with different colour combinations for striking results.

bootee cuties

MEASUREMENTS
The shoes will vary in size depending on the yarn
you choose. Using this pattern and yarn, the shoes
will fit 3–6 months

GATHER TOGETHER...
materials
Less than 1 x 1¾oz (50g) ball of any plain
or fancy light-weight (DK) polyester yarn (122yd/
112m per ball)

needles and notions
1 pair of size 6 (4mm) knitting needles for blue
fuzzy shoe, pink shoe and three-coloured shoe
1 pair of size 8 (5mm) knitting needles for blue
and white striped shoe
2 buttons

GAUGE
This will depend on the yarn you choose

*knit note Work a tension swatch before you start
so you can check the shoe size that your chosen
yarn will make.*

Stockinette stitch was used for the basic shoe pattern. The soles of all the
shoes are knitted in stockinette stitch with the striped patterns and variations
such as seed stitch used only on the top of the shoe. There is a knitted ridge
that separates the sole of the shoe from the top.

Knit your basic shoes...

Left shoe
Cast on 31 sts.
Sole of shoe
Row 1 Purl.
Row 2 K1, kfb, k12, kfb, k1, kfb, k12, kfb, k1. 35 sts.
Row 3 Purl.
Row 4 K1, kfb, k14, kfb, k1, kfb, k14, kfb, k1. 39 sts.
Row 5 Purl.
Row 6 K1, kfb, kfb, k14, kfb, kfb, k1, kfb, kfb, k14, kfb, kfb, k1. 47 sts.
Rows 7 and 8 Knit.
Row 9 Purl.
Repeat rows 8 and 9 three more times.
Row 16 K15, (skpo) 4 times, k1, (k2tog) 4 times, k15. 39 sts.
Row 17 Purl.
Row 18 Bind off 8 sts, k4, bind off 26 sts to end of row. Cut yarn and rejoin it to the 5 sts remaining on the needle.
Row 19 K5 (these 5 sts form strap).
Knit a further 19 rows (or to the required length).
Row 39 K2, yfd, k2tog, k1 (buttonhole).
Row 40 K5.
Repeat row 40 twice more.
Bind off.
Sew in end and sew up along the centre of the sole and up the back of the shoe.
Sew button on side of shoe.

Right shoe
Work as for left shoe until row 17.
Row 18 Bind off 26 sts, k4, bind off 8 sts to end of row. Cut yarn and rejoin it to the 5 sts remaining on the needle.
Row 19 K5 (these 5 sts form strap).
Work strap as for left shoe.

baby's new look

Lilac lovelies – Using size 6 (4mm) needles, work the basic shoe pattern until row 8, then use seed stitch for the body of the shoe and strap.

Blue and white stripes – Using size 8 (5mm) needles and blue yarn, work the basic shoe pattern until row 8, then start stripes using white for 2 rows followed by blue for 2 rows. Knit each row to produce a garter stitch fabric.

Burgundy three-coloured stripes

Left shoe

Using size 6 (4mm) needles and **A**, cast on 31 sts.

Sole of shoe

Row 1 Purl.

Row 2 K1, kfb, k12, kfb, k1, kfb, k12, kfb, k1. 35 sts.

Row 3 Purl.

Row 4 K1, kfb, k14, kfb, k1, kfb, k14, kfb, k1. 39 sts.

Row 5 Purl.

Row 6 K1, kfb, kfb, k14, kfb, kfb, k1, kfb, kfb, k14, kfb, kfb, k1. 47 sts.

Rows 7 and 8 Using **B**, knit.

Row 9 Using **A**, purl.

Row 10 Knit.

Row 11 Using **C**, purl.

Row 12 Knit.

Row 13 Using **A**, purl.

Row 14 Knit.

Row 15 Using **B**, purl.

Row 16 K15, (skpo) 4 times, k1, (k2tog) 4 times, k15. 39 sts.

Row 17 Using **A**, purl.

Row 18 Bind off 8 sts, k4, bind off 26 sts to end of row. Cut yarn and rejoin it to the 5 sts remaining on the needle.

Row 19 K5 (these 5 sts form strap).

Knit a further 19 rows (or to the required length).

Row 39 K2, yfd, k2tog, k1 (buttonhole).

Row 40 K5.

Repeat row 40 twice more.

Bind off.

Sew in end and sew up along the centre of sole and up the back of the shoe.

Sew button on side of shoe.

Right shoe

Work as for left shoe until row 17.

Row 18 Bind off 26 sts, k4, bind off 8 sts to end of row. Cut yarn and rejoin it to the 5 sts remaining on the needle.

Row 19 K5 (these 5 sts form strap).

Row 20 K5.

Work strap as for left shoe.

animal mittens

Babies and young children will love these pretty animal mittens with their favourite farmyard friends sitting happily on the wristband. The mittens are all knitted in a soft yarn with contrasting bands of blue and green to show the sky and grass. The animals are made using the Fair Isle technique so that they are part of the knitted structure. The features and legs are embroidered at the end to add an extra dimension. Here you will find a larger cheeky chick design to fit a child, as well as adorable sheep, robin and spider patterns suitable to fit a baby, but the patterns can easily be adapted to the size of your choice.

These mittens are both warm and fun – and the crochet chain string means you will never be hunting for a lost mitten.

DESIGN SECRETS UNRAVELLED...

I wanted to knit a pair of easy mittens which would be attractive to young children. I designed chicks, sheep, spiders and robins, which are knitted into the top of each mitten, sitting on green grass with a blue sky background. The round shape of the animals makes it easy to adapt the design by using different colours and textures of yarn. White circles are turned into sheep, brown circles into robins and black circles into spiders. You could even turn the circles into little faces and add hair and embroidered features. The design gives you scope to be inventive with both the design and the final embroidery.

YARN FOCUS

The mittens are knitted in an easy-wash yarn which means they are ideal for children's wear. Small quantities of yarn are used in the pattern around the wrist, making it perfect for using up left-over yarns from other projects.

animal mittens

MEASUREMENTS

6¾in (17cm) from the wrist to mitten top,
suitable for 3–4 years

GATHER TOGETHER...
materials

A 1 x 1¾oz (50g) ball of light-weight (DK) wool
yarn (113yd/104m per ball) in red
Less than 1 x 1¾oz (50g) ball of light-weight
(DK) wool yarn (113yd/104m per ball) in each of:

B blue

C green

D yellow

needles and notions

1 pair of size 6 (4mm) knitting needles

GAUGE

19 sts and 26 rows to 4in (10cm) over st st

The mittens are knitted in stockinette stitch with a garter stitch border. The increases which lead up to the thumbs form a pattern so you can easily see if you have made a mistake. Once the thumb has been knitted, sew it up. This makes it easier to see where to pick up the two extra stitches that form the top of the mitten. When knitting the Fair Isle circles, make sure you regularly link the coloured yarns around one another at the back. You don't want to end up with long loops which could get caught on little fingers when the child puts the mitten on.

Knit your large cheeky chick mittens...

Right mitten

Cast on 34 sts in **A**.
Rows 1 to 4 Knit.
Row 5 Using **B**, knit.
Row 6 Purl.
Start chicks
Row 7 K4**B**, (k2**D**, k6**B**) 3 times, k2**D**, k4**B**.
Row 8 P3**B**, (p4**D**, p4**B**) 3 times, p4**D**, p3**D**.
Row 9 K2**B**, (k6**D**, k2**B**) 3 times, k6**D**, k2**B**.
Row 10 P2**B**, (p6**D**, p2**B**) 3 times, p6**D**, p2**B**.
Row 11 K3**B**, (k4**D**, k4**B**) 3 times, k4**D**, k3**B**.
Row 12 P4**B**, (p2**D**, p6**B**) 3 times, p2**D**, p4**B**.
Row 13 Using **B**, knit.
Row 14 Purl.
Start thumb shaping
Row 15 Using **C**, k17, kfb, kfb, k15. 36 sts.
Row 16 Purl.
Row 17 Knit.
Row 18 Purl.
Row 19 Using **A**, k17, kfb, k2, kfb, k15. 38 sts.
Row 20 Purl.
Row 21 Knit.
Row 22 Purl.
Row 23 K17, kfb, k4, kfb, k15. 40 sts.
Row 24 Purl.
Row 25 Knit.
Row 26 Purl.
Row 27 K17, kfb, k6, kfb, k15. 42 sts.
Row 28 Purl.
Row 29 Knit.
Row 30 Purl.
Row 31 K27, turn.

Thumb
Thumb row 1 Kfb, p9, kfb. 13sts.
Work on these 13 sts in st st for 8 rows.
Thumb row 10 (K1, k2tog), rep to last st, k1. 9 sts.
Cut yarn, thread though sts and pull tight.
Sew up thumb seam.

Body of mitten
Join yarn at start of thumb.
Continuing with row 31 Pick up and knit 2 sts from base of thumb, k15 (to end of row).
Row 32 Purl.
Work in st st for 18 rows.
Row 51 (K1, k2tog), rep to last 2 sts, k2. 12 sts.
Row 52 Purl.
Row 53 (K2tog), rep to end. 6 sts.
Cut yarn, thread though sts and pull tight.

Left mitten
Knit as for the right mitten until row 15.
Start thumb shaping
Row 15 Using **C**, k14, kfb, kfb, k18. 36 sts.
Row 16 Purl.
Row 17 Knit.
Row 18 Purl.
Row 19 Using **A**, k14, kfb, k2, kfb, k18. 38 sts.
Row 20 Purl.
Row 21 Knit.
Row 22 Purl.
Row 23 K14, kfb, k4, kfb, k18. 40 sts.
Row 24 Purl.
Row 25 Knit
Row 26 Purl.

Row 27 K14, kfb, k6, kfb, k18. 42 sts.
Row 28 Purl.
Row 29 Knit.
Row 30 Purl.
Row 31 K24, turn.

Thumb

Thumb row 1 Kfb, p9, kfb. 13 sts.
Work on these 13 sts in st st for 8 rows.
Thumb row 10 (K1, k2tog), rep to last st, k1. 9 sts.
Cut yarn, thread though sts and pull tight.
Sew up thumb seam.

Body of mitten
Join yarn at start of thumb.
Continuing with row 31 Pick up and knit 2 sts from base of thumb, k18
(to end of row).
Row 32 Purl.
Continue as for right mitten.

To finish...
Sew in all loose ends.
Carefully sew up the seam from the top of the mitten to the wrist.
Embroider the chick's eyes, beaks and legs using fine yarn or embroidery thread.

You could make a string from crochet chain stitch in **A** to join the two mittens
together. The mittens could then be threaded through the sleeves of a jacket
to stop a mitten from getting lost.

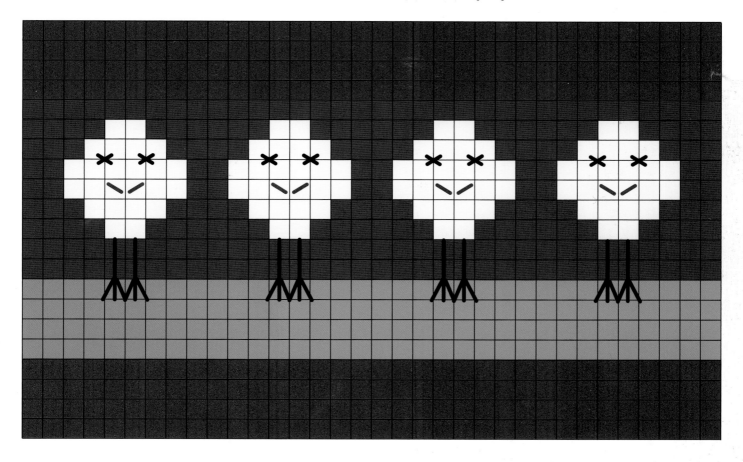

MEASUREMENTS

To fit size in months: 0–3
4¾in (12cm) from the wrist to mitten top

GATHER TOGETHER...
materials

A 1 x 1oz (25g) ball of light-weight (DK) polyester yarn (92yd/85m per ball) in dark green
Less than 1 x 1oz (25g) ball of light-weight (DK) polyester yarn (92yd/85m per ball) in each of:

B blue
C light green
D white

needles and notions

1 pair of size 6 (4mm) knitting needles

GAUGE

19 sts and 26 rows to 4in (10cm) over st st

Knit your small sheep mittens...

Right mitten

Cast on 26 sts in **A**.
Rows 1 to 4 Knit.
Row 5 Using **B**, knit.
Row 6 Purl.

Start sheep

Row 7 K4**B**, (k2**D**, k6**B**) twice, k2**D**, k4**B**.
Row 8 P3**B**, (p4**D**, p4**B**) twice, p4**D**, p3**B**.
Row 9 K2**B**, (k6**D**, k2**B**) twice, k6**D**, k2**B**.
Row 10 P2**B**, (p6**D**, p2**B**) twice, p6**D**, p2**B**.
Row 11 K3**B**, (k4**D**, k4**B**) twice, k4**D**, k3**B**.
Row 12 P4**B**, (p2**D**, p6**B**) twice, p2**D**, p4**B**.
Row 13 Using **B**, knit.
Row 14 Purl.

Start thumb shaping

Row 15 Using **C**, k13, kfb, kfb, k11. 28 sts.
Row 16 Purl.
Row 17 K13, kfb, k2, kfb, k11. 30 sts.
Row 18 Purl.
Row 19 Using **A**, k13, kfb, k4, kfb, k11. 32 sts.
Row 20 Purl.
Row 21 K13, kfb, k6, kfb, k11. 34 sts.
Row 22 Purl.
Row 23 K23, turn.

Thumb

Thumb row 1 Kfb, p7, kfb. 11 sts.
Work on these 11 sts in st st for 6 rows.
Thumb row 8 (K1, k2tog), rep to last 2 sts, k2. 8 sts.
Cut yarn, thread though sts and pull tight.

Sew up thumb seam.

Body of mitten

Join yarn at start of thumb.
Continuing with row 23 Pick up and knit 2 sts from base of thumb, k11 (to end of row).
Row 24 Purl.
Work in st st for 10 rows.
Row 35 (K1, k2tog), rep to last st, k1. 9 sts.
Row 36 Purl.
Row 37 (K2tog), rep to last st, k1. 5 sts.
Thread yarn though sts. Pull tight.

Left mitten

Knit as for the right mitten until row 15.

Start thumb shaping

Row 15 Using **C**, k10, kfb, kfb, k14. 28 sts.
Row 16 Purl.
Row 17 K10, kfb, k2, kfb, k14. 30 sts.
Row 18 Purl.
Row 19 Using **A**, k10, kfb, k4, kfb, k14. 32 sts.
Row 20 Purl.
Row 21 K10, kfb, k6, kfb, k14. 34 sts.
Row 22 Purl.
Row 23 K20, turn.

Thumb

Thumb row 1 Kfb, p7, kfb. 11 sts.
Work on these 11 sts in st st for 6 rows.
Thumb row 8 (K1, k2tog), rep to last 2 sts, k2. 8 sts.
Cut yarn, thread though sts and pull tight.
Sew up thumb seam.

Body of mitten

Join yarn at start of thumb.
Continuing with row 23 Pick up and knit 2 sts from base of thumb, k14 (to end of row).
Row 24 Purl.
Continue as for right mitten.

To finish...

Sew in all loose ends.
Carefully sew up the seam from the top of the mitten to the wrist. Embroider the sheep's eyes, nose and legs using fine yarn or embroidery thread.

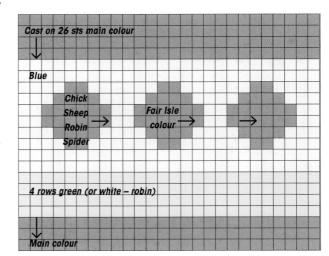

baby's new look

materials

Robin mittens

A 1 x 1¾oz (50g) ball of light-weight (DK) extra fine merino/acrylic microfibre/cashmere mix yarn (142yd/130m per ball) in pink

Less than 1 x 1¾oz (50g) ball of light-weight (DK) extra fine merino/acrylic microfibre/cashmere mix yarn (142yd/130m per ball) in each of:

B blue

C brown

D Less than 1 x 1oz (25g) ball of light-weight (DK) polyester yarn (92yd/85m per ball) in white

Spider mittens

A 1 x 1¾oz (50g) ball of light-weight (DK) nylon/acrylic mix yarn (191yd/175m per ball) in grey

Less than 1 x 1¾oz (50g) ball of light-weight (DK) nylon/acrylic mix yarn (191yd/175m per ball) in each of:

B blue

C light green

D black

Knit the spider and robin mittens in the same way as the sheep mittens (see page 28), substituting the white sheep yarn with the black yarn for the spider or the brown yarn for the robin.

When the mittens have been knitted, embroider black legs and yellow eyes on to the spider and a red breast, beak and eyes on to the robin.

lovely lacy set

This stunning set, comprising of hat, mittens and bootees is knitted using the same pretty lace pattern, is relatively easy to knit, and is suitable for both boys and girls. The set is knitted using a lovely soft cream yarn which allows the detail of the lace pattern to show through and is trimmed with ribbon, which could be coloured pink or blue if desired, to add that extra special touch. This set would be the perfect ensemble for baby's christening or would be a sweet little gift to celebrate a new baby's arrival.

The ribbon is both pretty and practical. Use ribbon in a contrasting colour to your yarn to give this set an extra zing.

DESIGN SECRETS UNRAVELLED...

I wanted to knit a set of baby accessories that incorporated a relatively easy lace pattern. You could use a number of yarns in a variety of colours to create a variety of looks; for example, cotton yarns in bright, lively colours would look brilliant for a summer set. I incorporated a series of eyelet holes to thread ribbon through in the mittens and bootees to help the items stay on little hands and feet. I used plain ribbon, but a fancier ribbon could add colour and decoration.

YARN FOCUS

I chose a plain light-weight yarn which shows the lace pattern of the hat, mittens and bootees clearly. It is extremely soft and therefore is perfect for a very young baby. A fluffy yarn would not give clarity to the pattern, so would not be as suitable for this design. As the whole set uses only two balls of yarn, you could go to the bargain bins for end-of-range balls to make an economical set of baby accessories.

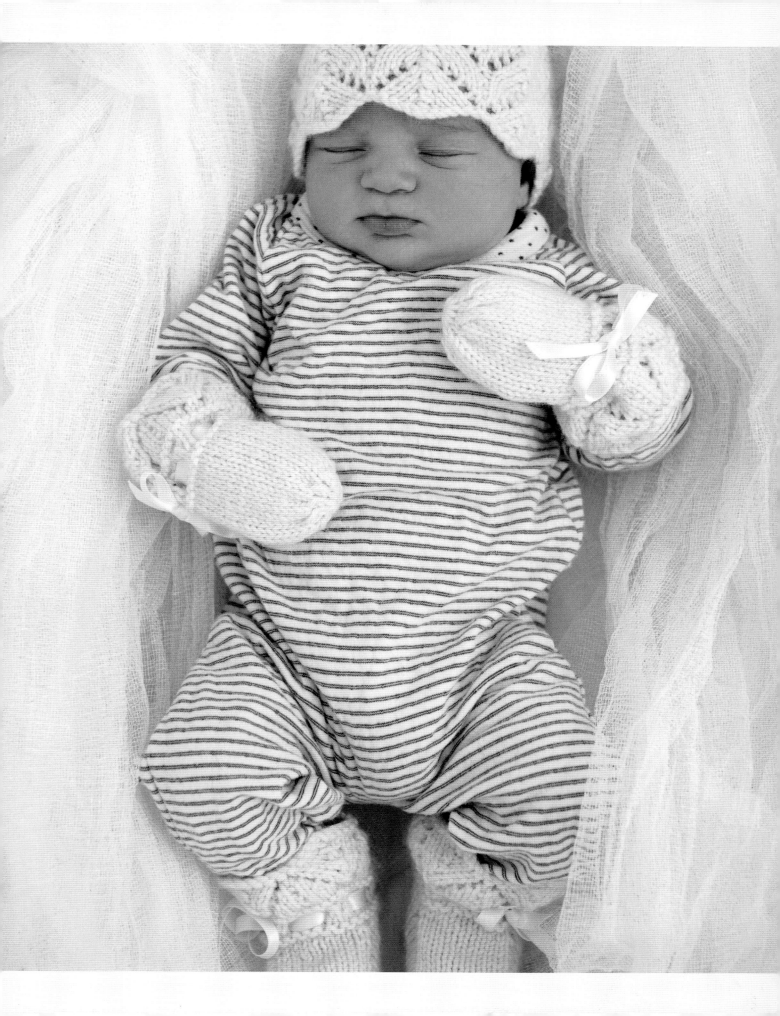

lovely lacy set

MEASUREMENTS

To fit size: newborn
Hat – 14⅛in (36cm) round head
x 4¾in (12cm) tall
Bootee – 3⅛in (8cm) tall x 3⅛in (8cm) long
Mittens – 4in (10cm) long

GATHER TOGETHER...
materials

2 x 1¾oz (50g) balls of light-weight (DK)
wool/microfibre/cashmere mix yarn
(142yd/130m per ball) in cream
Ribbon – ⅜in (1cm) wide x 15¾in (40cm) long

needles and notions

1 pair of size 6 (4mm) knitting needles

GAUGE

22 sts and 30 rows to 4in (10cm) over st st

knit note Keep track of which row of the pattern you need to work next by using a row counter, or write the row numbers on a piece of paper and tick them off as you work them.

This gorgeous set of hat, mittens and bootees incorporates a pattern that is knitted over 10 stitches and 8 rows which are repeated. It is easy to see the pattern forming once you have knitted a few rows, with the holes and the increases and decreases forming zigzags. You know immediately if you have made a mistake. Experiment with the size of the accessories by adding an extra 10 stitches for extra width or knitting an extra 8 rows for increased length.

Pattern (Horseshoe lace)
Consists of 10 sts plus 1 st and 8 rows

Row 1 and every following WS row Purl.
Row 2 (RS) K1, (yfd, k3, sl 1, k2tog, psso, k3, yfd, k1), repeat to end of row.
Row 4 P1, (k1, yfd, k2, sl 1, k2tog, psso, k2, yfd, k1, p1), repeat to end of row.
Row 6 P1, (k2, yfd, k1, sl 1, k2tog, psso, k1, yfd, k2, p1), repeat to end of row.
Row 8 P1, (k3, yfd, sl 1, k2tog, psso, yfd, k3, p1), repeat to end of row.

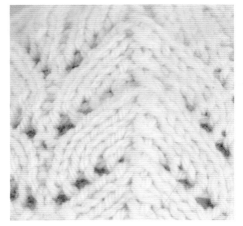

Knit your lovely lacy set...

Hat

Cast on 81 stitches leaving a length of yarn for sewing up.
Rows 1 to 8 Work 8 rows of pattern.
Repeat pattern 3 times.
Shape top
Row 24 and every following WS row Purl.
Row 25 and 27 K1, (k3, yfd, sl 1, k2tog, psso, yfd, k4), rep to end of row.
Row 29 K4, (yfd, sl 1, k2tog, psso, yfd, k2, sl 1, k2tog, psso, k2), rep to last 7 sts, yfd, sl 1, k2tog, psso, yfd, k1, sl 1, k2tog, psso. 65 sts.
Row 31 K4, (yfd, sl 1, k2tog, psso, yfd, k5), rep to last 5 sts, yfd, sl 1, k2tog, psso, yfd, k2.
Row 33 Sl 1, k2tog, psso, k1 (yfd, sl 1, k2tog, psso, yfd, k1, sl 1, k2tog, psso, k1), rep to last 5 sts, yfd, sl 1, k2tog, psso, yfd, k2. 49 sts.
Row 35 K2, (yfd, sl 1, k2tog, psso, yfd, k3), rep to last 5 sts, yfd, sl 1, k2tog, psso, yfd, k2.
Row 37 Skpo, (yfd, sl 1, k2tog, psso, yfd, sl 1, k2tog,

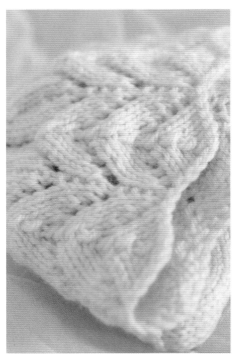

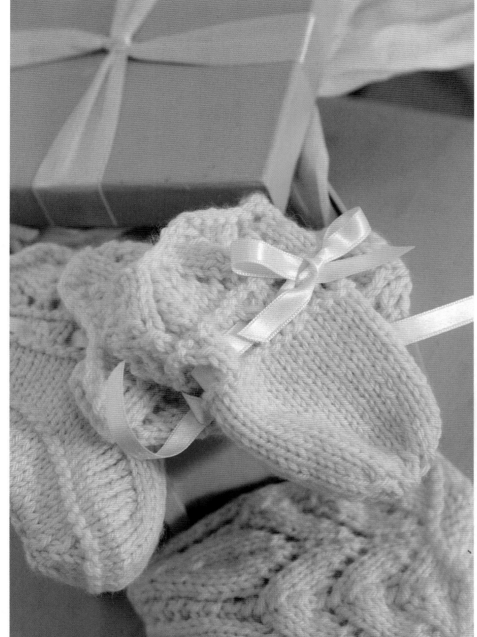

This pretty set makes an ideal gift for a new arrival and will suit either a boy or a girl.

psso), rep to last 5 sts, yf, sl 1, k2tog, psso, yfd, skpo. 33 sts.

Row 39 (Sl 1, k2tog, psso), rep to end of row. 11 sts. Cut yarn and thread it through sts.

To finish...

Sew back seam to form the hat.

Lace mittens (make 2)

Cast on 41 stitches.

Work 8 rows of horseshoe lace pattern (as for hat).

Row 9 Purl.

Rows 10, 11 and 12 Knit.

Row 13 Purl.

Row 14 (K1, yfd, sl 1, k2tog, psso), rep to last st, k1. 31sts.

Row 15 Purl.

Rows 16, 17 and 18 Knit.

Row 19 Purl.

Work in st st for 18 rows.

Row 38 (Sl 1, k2tog, psso), rep to last st, k1. 11 sts.

Row 39 Purl.

Cut yarn and thread it through stitches.

Thread ribbon through lace holes.

To finish...

Sew in ends. Sew up along seam.

Lace bootees (make 2)

Cast on 41 stitches.

Work 8 rows of horseshoe lace pattern (as for hat).

Row 9 Purl.

Row 10, 11 and 12 Knit.

Row 13 Purl.

Row 14 (K1, yfd, sl 1, k2tog, psso), repeat to last st, k1. 31sts.

Row 15 Purl.

Row 16, 17 and 18 Knit.

Row 19 Purl.

Top of bootee

Row 20 K21, turn.

Row 21 P11, turn.

Row 22 Sl 1, k10.

Row 23 Sl 1, p10.

Repeat rows 22 and 23 seven times to form the top of bootee. Cut off yarn and rejoin to beg of first 10 sts.

Sides of bootees

Row 38 Pick up and knit 9 sts from right side of bootee top, k 11, pick up and knit 9 sts from left side of bootee top, k remaining 10 sts. 49 sts.

Row 39 Purl.

Work in st st for 5 rows.

Row 45 Knit (to form ridge separating side from sole of bootee).

Sole of bootee

Row 46 K4, k2tog, k13, skpo, k7, k2tog, k13, skpo, k4.

Row 47 Purl.

Row 48 K4, k2tog, k11, skpo, k7, k2tog, k11, skpo, k4.

Row 49 Purl.

Row 50 (K2tog) 3 times, k9, (skpo) twice, k3, (k2tog) twice, k9, (skpo) three times. 31 sts. Bind off purlwise.

To finish...

Sew up along centre of bootee sole.

Thread ribbon through lace holes at the ankle.

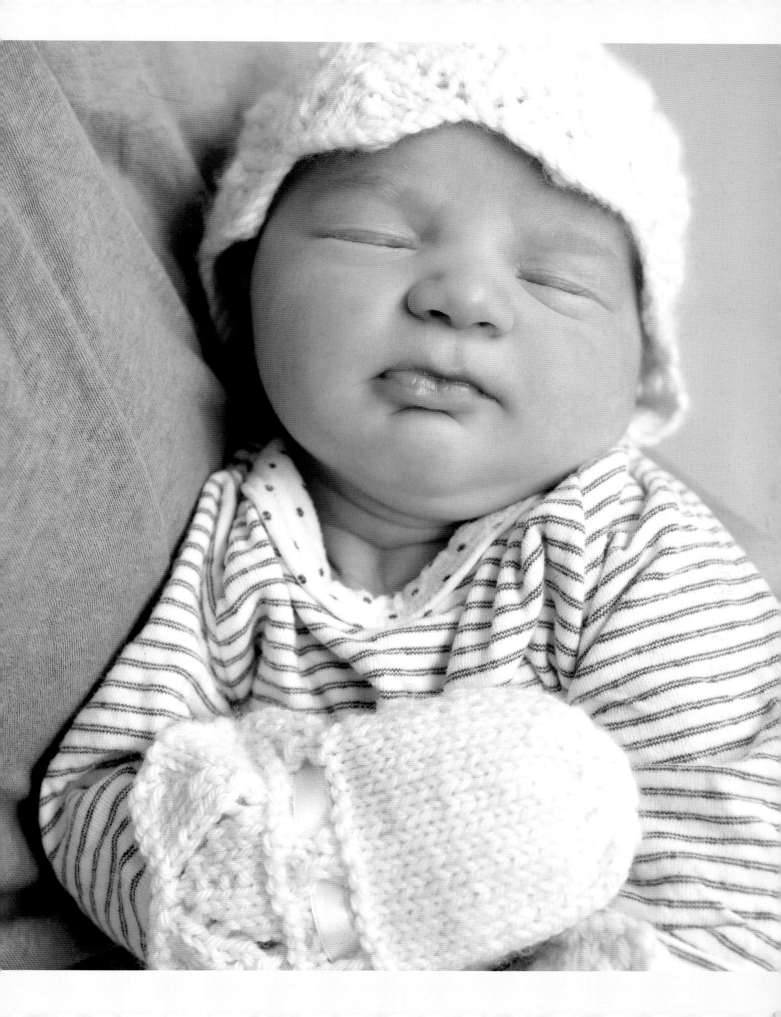

baby's new look

Although lace fabrics are traditionally knitted in white or pale colours, they look equally pretty in brighter colours. Using patterned or embroidered ribbon in contrasting colours can give a totally unique finish to your set. Or go for a dramatic look using black yarn and bright ribbon.

materials

Maroon mittens

Less than 1 x 3½oz (100g) of light-weight (DK) extra fine merino/acrylic microfibre/cashmere mix yarn (142yd/130m per ball) in maroon.

Marine mix mittens

Less than 1 x 3½oz (100g) balls of acrylic yarn (258yd/236m per ball) in pale green and blue.

Baby blue mittens

Less than 1 x 1¾oz (50g) ball of light-weight (DK) Cotton/Acrylic mix yarn (172yd/158m per ball) in pale blue.

Maroon mittens – Using size 6 (4mm) needles and maroon yarn, work the mitten pattern. Embellish with matching maroon ribbon.

Marine mix mittens – Using size 6 (4mm) needles, cast on 41 stitches in blue.

Work 8 rows of horseshoe lace pattern (as for hat).

Row 1 Purl.

Change to green for row 2 of pattern

Row 9 Purl.

Row 10–12 Using blue, knit.

Row 13 Purl.

Row 14 (k1, yfd, sl 1, k2tog, psso) repeat to last st, k1. 31sts.

Row 15 Purl.

Row 16–17 Knit

Row 18 Using green, knit.

Row 19 Purl.

Row 20–37 St st.

Row 38 (sl 1, k2tog, psso) repeat to last st, k1. 11 sts.

Row 39 Purl.

To finish...

Thread yarn through stitches. Sew in ends. Sew up along seam. Thread thick blue ribbon through lace holes.

Baby blue mittens – Using size 6 (4mm) needles and blue yarn, work the basic mitten pattern. Embellish by combining several thin white ribbons together.

bobbles and stripes set

This striking set of hat, mittens and bootees is knitted using bright red and blue yarn to form different thicknesses of stripes. The set is suitable for both boys and girls and would brighten up any dull winter's day. The design is simple to knit and can be embellished with brightly coloured ribbon to add detail. The fluffy bobble on top of the hat adds to the fun of the set and will ensure that your baby stands out from the crowd. This set would make a delightful gift for a baby born in the cold winter months, to ensure they stay warm and snug whilst out and about in their pram.

Stripe patterns are simple yet versatile, and ideally suited to creating cheerful clothes for your baby.

DESIGN SECRETS UNRAVELLED...

I wanted to knit a set of baby accessories that were bright and lively and stripes are perfect for this. I stuck to a palette of two colours, but you could use a variety of colours in different thicknesses of stripes. Alternatively you could stick to subdued colours to give a more subtle effect. The pompom on top of the hat uses just one of the colours, but it doesn't matter what colour you use or what size you make it. I have incorporated eyelet holes to thread ribbon through, but you may find that this is not necessary.

YARN FOCUS

I chose two colours of light-weight cotton to knit the hat, mittens and bootees. It is important when knitting baby hats and accessories to make sure that the yarn is soft. Fluffy yarns would work well in this design, as would soft woollen yarns. In fact the yarns you use depend only on the season you are knitting for.

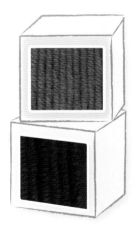

bobbles and stripes set

MEASUREMENTS

To fit size in months: 0–3
Hat – 13¾in (35cm) round head x 5in (13cm) tall
Bootee – 4in (10cm) long x 3in (7.5cm) tall
(rib not folded)
Mittens – 4¾in (12cm) long

GATHER TOGETHER...
materials
1 x 1¾oz (50g) ball of medium-weight (aran)
cotton/acrylic microfibre mix yarn (98yd/90m per
ball) in each of **A** red and **B** blue

needles and notions
1 pair of size 8 (5mm) knitting needles
Ribbon if required

GAUGE
18 sts and 25 rows to 4in (10cm)

knit note Make sure that when you knit the mittens and bootees, you knit either the optional lace hole row or the plain knit row. Don't knit an extra row by mistake!

This set of hat, mittens and bootees is very easy to make. All of the items start with a rib and then are worked in stockinette stitch. The stripes are knitted in multiples of two rows so that all the yarn ends start and finish on the same side. I did not cut the ends off when knitting, but looped them round one another to avoid having to sew them in, and to make a neater finish.

Knit your bobbles and stripes set...

Hat
Using **A**, cast on 72 sts.
Rows 1 to 8 K2, p2 rib.
Change to **B**.
Row 9 Knit.
Row 10 Purl.
Repeat rows 9 and 10 twice more.
Change to **A**.
Row 15 Knit.
Row 16 Purl.
Repeat rows 15 and 16 once.
Change to **B**.
Row 19 Knit.
Row 20 Purl.
Change to **A**.
Row 21 (K3, sl 1, k2tog, psso, k3), rep to end of row. 56 sts.
Row 22 Purl.

Row 23 Knit.
Row 24 Purl.
Row 25 (K2, sl 1, k2tog, psso, k2), rep to end of row. 40sts.
Row 26 Purl.
Change to **B**.
Row 27 Knit.
Row 28 Purl.
Row 29 (K1, sl 1, k2tog, psso, k1), rep to end of row. 24 sts.
Row 30 Purl.
Row 31 (Sl 1, k2tog, psso), rep to end of row. 8 sts.
Row 32 Purl.
Cut yarn and thread through sts.

To finish...
Sew in end and sew up along back seam.
See page 116 for instructions to make a pompom.
Sew to top of hat.

Mittens (make 2)

Using **A**, cast on 28 sts.

Rows 1 to 6 K2, p2 rib.

Change to **B**.

Row 7 Knit.

Row 8 Purl.

Row 9 Knit.

Optional lace hole row (Row 9) K1, (yfd, k2tog), rep to last st, k1.

Row 10 Purl.

Change to **A**.

Row 11 Knit.

Row 12 Purl.

Change to **B**.

Row 13 Knit.

Row 14 Purl.

Repeat these 2 rows once.

Change to **A**.

Row 17 Knit.

Row 18 Purl.

Repeat these 2 rows once.

Change to **B**.

Row 21 Knit.

Row 22 Purl.

Change to **A**.

Row 23 K1, (k3, sl 1, k2tog, psso, k3), rep to end of row. 22 sts.

Row 24 Purl.

Change to **B**.

Row 25 K1, (k2, sl 1, k2tog, psso, k2), rep to end of row. 16 sts.

Row 26 Purl.

Row 27 K1, (k1, sl 1, k2tog, psso, k1), rep to end of row. 10 sts.

Row 28 Purl.

Cut yarn and thread through sts.

To finish...

Sew in ends. Sew up along seam.

Bootees (make 2)

Using **A**, cast on 28 sts.

Rows 1 to 8 K2, p2 rib.

Change to **B**.

Row 9 Knit.

Row 10 Purl.

Row 11 Knit.

Optional lace hole row (Row 11) K1, (yfd, k2tog), rep to last st, k1.

Row 12 Purl.

Change to **A**.

Row 13 Knit.

Row 14 Purl.

Change to **B** for top of bootee.

Row 15 K19, turn.

Row 16 P10, turn.

Row 17 K10, turn.

Row 18 P10, turn.

Repeat rows 17 and 18 four times to form top of bootee.

Cut off yarn and rejoin to beg of first 9 sts.

Row 27 Using **B**, start from end of first 9 sts, pick up and knit 8 sts from right side of bootee top, k10, pick up and knit 8 sts from left side of bootee top, k remaining 9 sts. 44 sts.

Row 28 Purl.

Change to **A**.

Row 29 Knit.

Row 30 Purl.

Row 31 Knit.

Row 32 Knit (to form ridge separating side from sole of bootee).

Change to **B**.

Row 33 K3, k2tog, k12, skpo, k6, k2tog, k12, skpo, k3. 40 sts.

Row 34 Purl.

Row 35 (K2tog) 3 times, k10, (skpo) twice, (k2tog) twice, k10, (skpo) 3 times. 30 sts.

Row 36 Purl.

Bind off.

To finish...

Sew up centre of bootee sole.

baby's new look

It's amazing how colour choice can change the whole impact of this set. If you like an even bolder effect than red and blue, why not try a dramatic combination of navy blue and cerise? If you prefer pastel colours, then the set will look so pretty knitted in pastel blue and pink stripes. Or go for a fresh look with white, which will lift any colour combination. Mint green and cream also make a bright and happy spring colour combination.

materials

Spring green and cream
1 x 1¾oz (50g) ball of light-weight (DK) wool (114yd/104m per ball) in shades: **A** green and **B** cream.

Luscious lilac and taupe
1 x 1¾oz (50g) ball of light-weight (DK) extra fine merino/acrylic microfibre/cashmere mix yarn (142yd/130m per ball) in **A** lilac and **B** taupe.

Bold violet and blue
1 x 1¾oz (50g) ball of light-weight (DK)wool (114yd/104m per ball) in shades: **A** navy blue and **B** Violet.

so stripy sweater

This blue and white striped jumper is knitted from side to side rather than the conventional bottom to top method. This means that the stripes are vertical rather than horizontal. Similarly the sleeves are knitted round the arm rather than from wrist to armhole. The different directions of stripes give a bright and modern twist to a simple jumper design. I have used a traditional blue and cream colour scheme to suit a boy, but the pattern looks equally striking when knitted for a little girl in a pretty pink and cream colourway (see page 48).

Baby will look so smart in this sweater with its simple yet effective pattern.

YARN FOCUS

I chose two colours of soft light-weight wool. Fluffy yarns would work well in this design as would soft cotton yarns. You could even use yarns of different thicknesses which would accentuate the ridges formed by the garter stitch pattern.

DESIGN SECRETS UNRAVELLED...

I wanted to knit a simple, bright and lively jumper and stripes are perfect for this. I used garter stitch for the whole of the jumper – even the plain blue edging is knitted in garter stitch. The body of the jumper is knitted in one piece, casting on and binding off for the armholes and neck.

I used only two colours but you could use a variety of colours in different thicknesses of stripes as long as you use multiples of two rows for each colour. When changing from one colour to the other you need to make sure you are consistent with the way you wrap one colour round the other so that the edges of the jumper are neat.

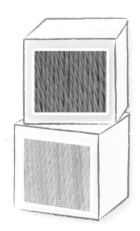

so stripy sweater

MEASUREMENTS
To fit size in months: 6–12
Actual chest measurement: 9⅞in (25cm)
Length: 10½in (27cm)

GATHER TOGETHER...
materials
2 x 1¾oz (50g) balls of light-weight (DK)
extra fine merino/acrylic microfibre/cashmere
mix yarn (142yd/130m per ball) in each of
A cream and **B** blue

needles and notions
1 pair of size 8 (5mm) knitting needles
Size 6 (4mm) circular needle or 4 double-pointed
needles for neck stitches
2 poppers

GAUGE
22 sts and 30 rows to 4in (10cm)

The sweater is knitted from the side so that the stripes are vertical. You start from the right side of the front, casting on stitches to form the armhole, carrying along the shoulder top, decreasing a few stitches for the neck and increasing for the other shoulder. This increasing and decreasing carries on for the whole of the body of the sweater, so you end up with a very long knitted structure which you fold to form the body. It is easy to knit but making it up is slightly more complicated, however it is well worth the effort. Care has to be taken fitting in the sleeves and picking up stitches from around the neck.

Knit your so stripy sweater...

Using **B**, cast on 30 sts.
Row 1 Knit.
Rows 2 and 3 Using **A**, knit.
Rows 4 and 5 Using **B**, knit.
Rows 6 and 7 Using **A**, knit.
Row 8 Using **B**, k30, cast on 25 sts.
Continue knitting in two-row stripes on these 55 sts for 20 rows.
Row 29 Using **B**, knit.
Row 30 Bind off 5 sts, k50.
Continue in two-row stripes on these 50 sts for 42 rows.
Row 73 Using **B**, k50, cast on 5 sts.

Row 74 Knit.
Continue knitting in two-row stripes on these 55 sts for 20 rows.
Row 95 Using **B**, knit.
Row 96 Bind off 25 sts, k to end of row.
Continue in two-row stripes on these 30 sts for 14 rows (under arm).
Row 111 Using **B**, k30, cast on 25 sts.
Row 112 Knit.
Continue in two-row stripes on these 55 sts for 82 rows (back of sweater).
Row 194 Using **B**, knit.
Row 195 Bind off 25 sts, k30.
Continue in two-row stripes for 7 rows.
Bind off.

Pay attention when sewing up this sweater so that it looks neat and smart.

Sleeves (knitted from armhole to wrist)

Using **B**, cast on 40 sts.

Row 1 Knit.

Rows 2 and 3 Using **A**, knit.

Rows 4 and 5 Using **B**, knit.

Continue in two-row stripes for 90 more rows or until the folded sleeve fits into the armhole.

Bind off.

To finish...

Join together the seam under the right arm (fold right sides together and carefully back stitch). Sew up the right shoulder carefully matching stripes. Do not sew left shoulder as you will be picking up stitches around the neck and across the shoulder to make an opening. Do not sew sleeve seams.

Neck edging and opening

Using **B**, pick up 64 sts round the neck and across the back to the edge of sleeve using a circular needle or four double-pointed needles.

Starting from the right side, knit across 64 sts (32 sts from front of jumper and 32 sts from back of jumper). When you get to the straight edges,

pick up 1 st from a white stripe and 1 st from a blue stripe all the way around.
Starting from the right side knit across the 64 sts.
Knit a further 4 rows.
Bind off loosely.

Top of shoulder

Using **B**, pick up 14 sts across the left shoulder and edging.
Starting from the right side knit across the 14 sts.
Knit a further 4 rows.
Bind off.

Fold the arms in half and position inside the armholes. Stab stitch the sleeves in place. Turn the sweater inside out and back stitch the rest of the sleeve to the under arm of the sweater and then along the arm seam.

Sew 2 poppers to the opening.

baby's new look

I knitted the sweater in a pink light-weight yarn and a cream fine cotton yarn to give texture and to create a pretty little jumper to suit a girl. Substitute the pink yarn for the blue and the cream for the white. I used size 6 (4mm) needles for both yarns.

When you finish knitting, before you sew up the sweater, look at the back side of the work. You might prefer the look of the back side which is more muted and subtle. If you prefer this side, make up the sweater with this side showing.

materials
Pretty in pink
2 x 1¾oz (50g) balls of light-weight (DK) extra fine merino/acrylic microfibre/cashmere mix yarn (142yd/130m per ball) in **A** pink
2 x 1¾oz (50g) balls of fine (4 ply) cotton yarn (186yd/170m per ball) in **B** cream

simple hooded cardigan

This pretty blue hooded cardigan is knitted using a bulky-weight yarn so it is lovely and warm. The thick yarn is knitted using large needles, making it very quick to knit. I used a single large button to fasten the cardigan and you can choose an eye-catching button design if you want to add detail to this simple garment. The cardigan is so simple and versatile – it can be knitted in any colour and will go with every outfit in your baby's wardrobe. Use the softest yarn you can find so that the cardigan will be kind to delicate skin and make your baby extra-huggable!

Adding a hood to this cardigan means your baby will stay extra snug through any cold spells.

DESIGN SECRETS UNRAVELLED...

I wanted to knit a simple baby's cardigan for beginner knitters. I used stockinette stitch for the bulk of the cardigan and created the hems, front side edges and edges of the hood border by purling on what would normally be a knit row. This forms a neat decorative ridge. The cardigan could be worn casually over dungarees or as a warm jacket over smarter clothes. You could even use it as a dressing gown.

YARN FOCUS

The beauty of a thick, bulky-weight yarn is that it knits up very quickly. In fact this cardigan could be made in a couple of evenings. Because the yarn is soft, it is suitable for very young babies. Any chunky yarn could be used to knit the cardigan. Some bulky-weight yarns are made from two colours to give a tweed effect and these yarns would be ideal for this cardigan. You can also make your own tweed effect by knitting together four different coloured light-weight yarns, or use fine yarns to create a totally unique design.

simple hooded cardigan

MEASUREMENTS
To fit size in months: 6–12
Actual chest measurement: 12in (30cm)
10½in (27cm) from bottom to top of shoulder
17¼in (44cm) from bottom to top of hood

GATHER TOGETHER...
materials
4 x 1¾oz (50g) balls of bulky (chunky) wool/
acrylic mix yarn (45yd/45m per ball) in blue

needles and notions
1 pair of size 13 (9mm) knitting needles
1 size 13 (9mm) circular needle
1 button

GAUGE
15 sts and 10 rows to 4in (10cm) over st st

The cardigan is very easy to knit, only using stockinette stitch with simple purl stitch borders. The decreases on raglan sleeves are made one stitch from the edges in order to make a feature of the shaping. Be careful when sewing the garment up; because the yarn is so chunky, using back stitch would make the seams bulky. I placed the seams together and made a neat linking stitch to join one knitted stitch to the other.

Knit your simple hooded cardigan...

Back
Cast on 30 sts.
Row 1 (WS) Purl.
Rows 2 and 3 As row 1.
Row 4 Knit.
Row 5 Purl.
Repeat the last 2 rows 4 times.
Row 14 K2tog, k26, k2tog. 28 sts.
Row 15 Purl.
Row 16 Knit.
Row 17 Purl.

Repeat the last 2 rows 4 times.
Shaping raglan armholes
Row 26 Bind off 2sts, k to end. 26 sts.
Row 27 Bind off 2sts, p to end. 24 sts.
Row 28 K1, skpo, k18, k2tog, k1. 22 sts.
Row 29 Purl.
Row 30 K1, skpo, k16, k2tog, k1. 20 sts.
Row 31 Purl.
Continue decreasing in this way until
10 sts remain.
Transfer sts to a holder.

Right side

Cast on 18 sts.

Row 1 (WS) Purl.

Rows 2 and 3 As row 1.

Row 4 P3, k15.

Row 5 Purl.

Repeat the last 2 rows 4 times.

Row 14 P3, k13, k2tog. 16 sts.

Row 15 Purl.

Row 16 P3, k14.

Row 17 Purl.

Repeat the last 2 rows 4 times.

Shaping raglan armholes

Row 26 P3, k14.

Row 27 Bind off 2 sts, p to end. 14 sts.

Row 28 P3, k9, k2tog, k1. 13 sts.

Row 29 Purl.

Row 30 P3, k8, k2tog, k1. 12 sts.

Row 31 Purl.

Continue decreasing in this way until 8 sts remain.

Transfer sts to a holder.

Left side

Cast on 18 sts.

Row 1 (WS) Purl.

Rows 2 and 3 As row 1.

Row 4 K15, p3.

Row 5 Purl.

Repeat the last 2 rows 4 times.

Row 14 K2tog, k13, p3. 16 sts.

Row 15 Purl.

Row 16 K14, p3.

Row 17 Purl.

Repeat the last 2 rows 4 times.

Shaping raglan armholes

Row 26 Bind off 2sts, k12, p3. 14 sts.

Row 27 Purl.

Row 28 K1, skpo, k to last 3 sts, p3. 13 sts.

Row 29 Purl.

Row 30 K1, skpo, k to last 3 sts, p3. 12 sts.

Row 31 Purl.

Continue decreasing in this way until

9 sts remain.

Buttonhole

Row 37 Purl.

Row 38 K1, skpo, k to last 3 sts, p1, ybwd, p2tog. 8 sts.

Row 39 Purl.

Transfer sts to a holder.

Sleeve (make 2)

Cast on 18 sts.

Rows 1, 2 and 3 Purl.

Row 4 Knit.

Row 5 Purl.

Repeat rows 4 and 5.

Row 8 Kfb, k16, kfb.

Row 9 Purl

Repeat rows 4 to 9 twice more. 24 sts.

Row 22 Knit.

Row 23 Purl.

Repeat rows 22 and 23.

Shaping raglan armholes

Row 26 Bind off 2 sts, k to end of row. 22 sts.

Row 27 Bind off 2 sts, p to end of row. 20 sts.

Row 28 K1, skpo, k14, k2tog, k1. 18 sts.

Row 29 Purl.

Row 30 K1, skpo, k12, k2tog, k1. 16 sts.

Row 31 Purl.

Continue deceasing in this way until 8 sts remain.

Row 39 Purl.

Transfer sts to a holder.

To finish...

Sew sleeve raglan edges to back and front raglan edges.

Sew up sleeve and side seams.

Neck shaping and hood

With right sides facing and using a size 13 (9mm) circular needle for flexibility, pick up stitches from the holders as follows: 8 sts from right side, 8 sts from top of sleeve, 10 sts

from back, 8 sts from top of sleeve, 8 sts from left side. 42 sts.

Neck – start on the right (knit) side
Using size 13 (9mm) needles:
Row 1 (of hood) (RS) P3, k2, k2tog, k1, k2tog, k4, skpo, K1, skpo, k4, k2tog, k1, k2tog, k4, skpo, k1, skpo, k2, p3. 34 sts.
Row 2 Purl.
Hood increases
Row 3 P3, k1, (kfb, k3) 3 times, kfb, kfb, (k3, kfb) 3 times, k1, p3. 42 sts.
Row 4 Purl.
Row 5 P3, k36, p3.
Row 6 Purl.
Repeat the last two rows 8 times.

Top of hood shaping
Row 23 P3, k26, turn.
Row 24 P2tog, p14, turn.
Row 25 Skpo, k12, k2tog, turn.
Row 26 Sl 1, p12, p2tog, turn.
Row 27 Sl 1, k12, k2tog, turn.
Row 28 Sl 1, p12, p2tog, turn.
Continue to decrease in this way until you reach the 3 st purl border, turn.
Next row Sl 1, bind off 14 sts and purl remaining 2 sts. Work 18 purl rows on 3 sts to reach remaining 3 sts.
Bind off, joining together purlwise.

Neatly sew band on to front of hood.
Sew in any yarn ends. Sew a button on right-hand side to correspond to the buttonhole.

baby's new look

To make a pinky brown tweed yarn, knit together four strands of light-weight yarns and follow the pattern for the simple hooded cardigan. The final result is as unique as the baby you are knitting for.

These colours are perfect for a baby girl and if you are knitting for a little surprise, you can substitute the yarns with creams and yellows.

materials
Sugar and spice
2 x 1¾oz (50g) balls of light-weight (DK) extra fine merino/microfibre/cashmere mix yarn (142yd/130m per ball) in each of dark pink, light pink and cream
2 x 1¾oz (50g) balls of light-weight (DK) merino yarn (137yd/125m per ball) in brown

pretty pinafore dress

As a child I had a little pinafore dress knitted by my grandmother, which I wore all the time and adored. It has given me inspiration for this simple yet striking design. The main detail of the pinafore is in the bodice section, created by knitting a 'garter slip stitch' pattern in three different coloured yarns. The few rows of coloured detail on the skirt pick up on the colours used in the bodice to enhance the design. I have knitted this dress in soft muted purples and pinks, however by changing the colour combinations it is easy to adapt the dress for any occasion or any time of the year.

Whatever colour combinations you choose, any little girl will look adorable in this pretty dress.

DESIGN SECRETS UNRAVELLED...

I have designed this little pinafore dress as a 'day dress', suitable for everyday wear. If you wanted to make it for a special occasion, you could use a yarn with bit of glitter, soft wool or luxurious cashmere. You could even experiment with different textures in the bodice.

The colours I used are muted and can be worn in either summer or winter, but you could experiment by using bright and bold colours or really pale soft pastel shades.

YARN FOCUS

I have knitted this little pinafore dress using a soft cotton yarn. Cotton is an ideal yarn for this design as it is light in weight, has a lovely drape and is very hard-wearing, making it ideal for a young adventurous child.

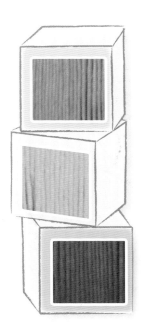

pretty pinafore dress

MEASUREMENTS
To fit size in months: 0–3
Actual chest measurement: 8in (20cm)
Length from hem to end of bodice pattern:
9⅞in (25cm)

GATHER TOGETHER...
materials
Light-weight (DK) 100% cotton yarn (104yd/95m
per 1¾oz (50g) ball) in the following colours:
A 2 balls in purple
B 1 ball in pink
C 1 ball in light purple

needles and notions
1 pair of size 6 (4mm) knitting needles
2 buttons

GAUGE
22 sts and 28 rows to 4in (10cm)

knit note *When you pick up the stitches around
the armholes and top of the dress, use the
bodice texture pattern to help you pick up the
stitches evenly.*

Unlike many dresses, this one is knitted starting from the bodice and working down towards the hem. This enables you to knit the most complicated part first and to knit the skirt to whatever length you like. You can also alter the length of the straps to fit the child. 'Garter slip stitch' is a very versatile pattern. I have used three different colours to form the pattern but you could use more or fewer. The very simple 'knit and purl' pattern at the bottom used as detail adds texture as well as emphasising the additional colours. You could add more rows of pattern to the skirt to add extra interest.

Knit your pinafore dress...

Back and front (make 2)
Bodice
Using **A**, cast on 31 sts.
Rows 1 and 2 Knit.
Row 3 Using **C**, k1, (sl 1 purlwise, k1), rep to end of row.
Row 4 K1, (yf, sl 1 purlwise, yb, k1), rep to end of row.
Rows 5 and 6 Using **B**, knit.
Row 7 Using **A**, k2, (sl 1 purlwise, k1), rep to last st, k1.
Row 8 K2, (yf, sl 1 purlwise, yb, k1), rep to last st, k1.
Repeat rows 1 to 8 twice changing the colour every two rows.
Row 25 Using **A**, kfb into first and last st of pattern.
Row 26 Knit.
Row 27 Using **C**, kfb, (sl 1 purl wise, k1) repeat to last 2 sts, sl 1, kfb.
Row 28 k2, (yf, sl 1 purl wise, yb, k1) rep to last st, k1.
Row 29 Using **B**, kfb, k to last st, kfb.
Row 30 Knit.
Row 31 Using **A**, kfb, (sl 1 purl wise, k1) rep to last 2 sts, sl 1, kfb.
Row 32 K2, (yf, sl 1 purl wise, yb, k1) rep to last st, k1
Cont with pattern and colour changes, increasing every other row to 47sts.

Middle band

Rows 41 to 46 Using **A**, knit.

Row 47 (Increase for skirt) k1, kfb, (k2, kfb), rep to end. 63 sts.

Row 48 Purl.

Work in st st for 50 rows ending with a p row.

Row 99 (would usually be a k row) Using **C**, purl.

Row 100 Knit.

Rows 101 and 102 Using **B**, knit.

Rows 103 and 104 Using **C**, knit.

Row 105 Using **A**, purl.

Work in st st for 4 rows.

Row 110 Purl.

Row 111 Knit.

Row 112 Purl.

Bind off.

To finish...

Sew in ends. Sew up seams.

Armhole edging (make 2)

Using **A**, pick up 21 sts from the top of the patterned bodice to the armhole seam on each side. 42 sts.

Knit across the 42 sts for 3 rows.

Bind off.

Straps (make 2)

Using **A**, pick up 8 sts from each end of the top back.

K on each set of 8 sts for 34 rows (or to the required length).

Row 35 (Buttonhole) K3, bind off 2 sts, k3.

Row 36 K3, cast on 2 sts, k3.

Knit 3 more rows.

Bind off.

Sew in yarn ends and attach buttons to the top edge of the front to match the buttonholes.

baby's new look

This is such a versatile pattern that you can use to make a pretty dress for any occasion. Cotton and wool/acrylic mix yarns will work well for an everyday dress that will go through a lot of wear and tear. But for a special occasion garment, why not consider using textured yarns in the bodice pattern to give added interest. Metallic yarns would add a glamorous touch of sparkle too.

Here I have designed a red and green dress, perfect to adorn your little one on Christmas day, a very soft, pretty pink dress to show off your little lady's feminine charm and a blue and green colourway for your little tomboy. If you do choose more exclusive yarns for a special project, do take care to read the washing instructions on the ball band as these yarns may require more careful laundering. I always try to use the same thickness yarn to ensure that the pattern comes up in a similar size each time.

materials

Festive feel

Light-weight (DK) pure wool yarn (114yd/104m per 1¾oz (50g) ball) in the following colours:

A 2 balls in cranberry
B 1 ball in green
C 1 ball in blue

Strawberries and cream

Light-weight (DK) extra fine merino/acrylic microfibre/cashmere mix yarn (142yd/130m per 1¾oz (50g) ball) in the following colours:

A 2 balls in cream
B 1 ball in dark pink
C 1 ball in light pink

Beautiful blues

Light-weight (DK) polyester yarn (92yd/85m per 1¾oz (50g) ball) in the following colours:

A 2 balls in light blue
B 1 ball in cream
C 1 ball in blue

peekaboo pocket cardigan

I love this cardigan with its sweet little teddy bear in the pocket, always on hand for your little one to play with. I was inspired by traditional Fair Isle knitwear, but I have given this cardigan a modern twist by using a simple knit and purl, three-colour pattern for the yoke. This pattern is repeated in the pocket detail. The little teddy is the perfect size to fit in the pocket and is attached by a thread so that it doesn't get lost. The cardigan could be worn by girls or boys depending on the colours and yarns you choose.

Baby will just love the surprise of finding teddy always to hand in his pocket!

YARN FOCUS

I have knitted this cardigan using two strands of a fine woollen yarn. Alternatively you could use a light weight yarn and use a single strand to give you the same effect. You could experiment by using a fluffy or glittery yarn in the yoke pattern to make a really elaborate cardigan. The teddy could be knitted to match.

DESIGN SECRETS UNRAVELLED...

I have designed this cardigan to enhance any outfit. It can be worn over dungarees or a smart dress. It has two main focuses: the yoke and the bear in the pocket. The texture in the yoke has been created by knitting on a purl row combined with a careful use of colour.

I have knitted in pinks, purple and greens which combine perfectly with the grey body of the cardigan. You could change these colours to suit the season or match an outfit.

The bear is the second focus and is knitted without too many extra parts to sew up. It is an ideal opportunity to experiment with colour and texture... but be careful to make sure he still fits in the pocket!

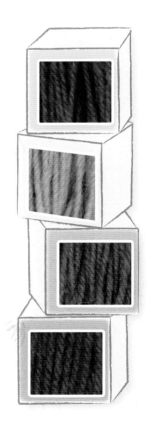

peekaboo pocket cardigan

MEASUREMENTS
To fit size in months: 3–6
Actual chest measurement: 11in (28cm)
Length: 11in (28cm)

GATHER TOGETHER...
materials
2 x 1¾oz (50g) balls of fine (4ply) wool/
polyamide mix yarn (224yd/205m per ball)
in each of **A** lilac and **B** grey
1 x 1¾oz (50g) ball of fine (4ply) wool/polyamide
mix yarn (224yd/205m per ball) in each of
C olive green and **D** mauve
Less than 1 x 3½oz (100g) ball of light-weight
(DK) yarn (325yd/298m per ball) or any yarn
oddment in pale blue for bear.

needles and notions
1 pair of size 6 (4mm) knitting needles
1 size 6 (4mm) circular needle
8 buttons
Small amount of stuffing and embroidery thread
for bear

GAUGE
22 sts and 33 rows to 4in (10cm)

knit note *If you are working with two strands
of yarn at the same time, make sure you work
through both strands for each stitch.*

Start at the bottom and work up, knitting the yoke in one piece once the back, sides and arms have all been sewn together. There are a lot of stitches when you reach the yoke and join all the parts together. It is easier to knit this on a circular needle because is has flexibility, but it can be used in a conventional 'straight' needle way; turning your work at the end of each row.

Knit your peekaboo pocket cardigan...

Back
Cast on 60 sts in **A**.
Row 1 *K1, p1; rep from * to end of row.
Row 2 *P1, k1; rep from * to end of row.
Rep these 2 rows 5 times.
Change to **B**.
Row 11 Knit.
Row 12 Purl.
Rep these 2 rows until work measures 7in (18cm) ending on a k row.
Shape armhole
Bind off 4 sts at beg of next 2 rows. 52 sts.
Leave sts on a holder to pick up later.

Right side
Cast on 30 sts in **A**.
Row 1 *K1, p1; rep from * to end of row.
Row 2 *P1, k1; rep from * to end of row.
Rep these 2 rows 5 times.
Change to **B**.
Row 11 Knit.
Row 12 Purl.
Rep these 2 rows until work measures 7in (18cm) ending on a knit row.
Shape armhole
Bind off 4 sts at beg of purl row. 26 sts.
Leave sts on a holder to pick up later.

Left side
Cast on 30 sts in **A**.
Row 1 *K1, p1; rep from * to end of row.
Row 2 *P1, k1; rep from * to end of row.
Rep these 2 rows 5 times.
Change to **B**.
Row 11 Knit.
Row 12 Purl.
Rep these 2 rows until work measures 7in (18cm) ending on a purl row (1 row less than right side).
Shape armhole
Bind off 4 sts at beg of knit row. 26 sts.
Purl 1 row.
Leave sts on a holder to pick up later.

Sleeves (make 2)
Cast on 36 sts in **A**.
Row 1 *K1, p1; rep from * to end of row.
Row 2 *P1, k1; rep from * to end of row.
Rep these 2 rows 5 times.
Change to **B**.
Row 11 Knit.
Row 12 Purl.
Repeat these 2 rows twice.
Row 17 Inc 1 st at start and end of row. 38 sts.
Continue increasing in the same way every foll 6th row until you have 44 sts.
Continue in st st until sleeve measures 7in (18cm).
Shape top:
Bind off 4 sts at beg of next 2 rows. 36 sts.
Leave sts on a holder to pick up later.

Yoke

With right sides facing forward and using a size 6 (4mm) circular needle and **B**, knit across stitches on holders for right front (26 sts), sleeve (36 sts), back (52 sts), sleeve (36 sts) and left front (26 sts). 176 sts.

Row 1 (WS) Using **A**, knit. (This should be a purl row but you change it to a k row to add texture.)

Row 2 K23, k2tog, k2, skpo, k30, k2tog, k2, skpo, k46, k2tog, k2, skpo, k30, k2tog, k2, skpo, k23. 168 sts.

Row 3 Purl.

Row 4 K22, k2tog, k2, skpo, k28, k2tog, k2, skpo, k44, k2tog, k2, skpo, k28, k2tog, k2, skpo, k22. 160 sts.

Row 5 Using **B**, knit.

Row 6 K21, k2tog, k2, skpo, k26, k2tog, k2, skpo, k42, k2tog, k2, skpo, k26, k2tog, k2, skpo, k21. 152 sts.

Row 7 Using **C**, knit.

Row 8 K20, k2tog, k2, skpo, k24, k2tog, k2, skpo, k40, k2tog, k2, skpo, k24, k2tog, k2, skpo, k20. 144 sts.

Row 9 Purl.

Row 10 K19, k2tog, k2, skpo, k22, k2tog, k2, skpo, k38, k2tog, k2, skpo, k22, k2tog, k2, skpo, k19. 136 sts.

Row 11 Using **A**, purl.

Row 12 K18, k2tog, k2, skpo, k20, k2tog, k2, skpo, k36, k2tog, k2, skpo, k20, k2tog, k2, skpo, k18. 128 sts.

Row 13 Using **D**, knit.

Row 14 K17, k2tog, k2, skpo, k18, k2tog, k2, skpo, k34, k2tog, k2, skpo, k18, k2tog, k2, skpo, k17. 120 sts.

Row 15 Purl.

Row 16 K16, k2tog, k2, skpo, k16, k2tog, k2, skpo, k32, k2tog, k2, skpo, k16, k2tog, k2, skpo, k16. 112 sts.

Row 17 Using **A**, knit.

Row 18 K15, k2tog, K2, skpo, k14, k2tog, k2, skpo, k30, k2tog, k2, skpo, k14, k2tog, k2, skpo, k15. 104 sts.

Row 19 Using **C,** knit.

Row 20 K14, k2tog, k2, skpo, k12, k2tog, k2, skpo, k28, k2tog, k2, skpo, k12, k2tog, k2, skpo, k14. 96 sts.

Row 21 Purl.

Row 22 K13, k2tog, k2, skpo, k10, k2tog, k2, skpo, k26, k2tog, k2, skpo, k10, k2tog, k2, skpo, k13. 88 sts.

Row 23 Using **B**, knit.

Row 24 K12, k2tog, k2, skpo, k8, k2tog, k2, skpo, k24, k2tog, k2, skpo, k8, k2tog, k2, skpo, k12. 80 sts.

Row 25 Using **A**, Knit.

Row 26 *K1, p1; rep from * to end of row.

Row 27 *P1, k1; rep from * to end of row.

Row 28 As row 26.

Row 29 K1, p1 for 13 sts, p3tog, k1, p1 for 9 sts, p3tog, k1, p1 for 25 sts, p3tog, k1, p1 for 9 sts, p3tog, k1, p1 to end of row. 72 sts.

Rows 30 and 31 As rows 26 and 27.

Bind off knitwise.

To finish...

After you have knitted the yoke, sew up the underarms (the 4 sts bound off). Then sew from the base of cardigan all the way up the sides to the underarm and down to the sleeve, keeping the colours consistent (sew grey sections with **A**, lilac sections with **B** and so on.) Carefully sew in the ends of the yarn. This must be done before the ribbed edging is started.

Ribbed edging – left side

Using **A**, pick up 8 sts from the bottom rib, 34 sts from the st st section, 14 sts from the yoke and 6 sts from the top rib. 62 sts.
Starting from neck edge, work in k1, p1 rib for 6 rows.
Bind off purlwise.

Ribbed edging – right side

Using **A**, pick up 6 sts from top rib, 14 sts from the yoke, 34 sts from the st st section, 8 sts from the bottom rib. 62 sts.
Row 1 Starting from bottom, p1, k1; rep to end of row.
Row 2 P1, k1 cont to end of row.
Row 3 P1, k1, yf, k2tog, *p1, k1, p1, k1, p1, k1, yf, k2tog, rep from * to last 2 sts, p1, k1.
Row 4 P1, k1, cont to end of row.
Row 5 P1, k1 cont to end of row.
Row 6 P1, k1 cont to end of row.
Bind off.

Pocket

Cast on 20 sts in **B**.

Work 14 rows in st st.

Row 15 Using **A**, knit.

Row 16 Using **D**, knit.

Row 17 Using **C**, purl.

Row 18 Using **A**, knit.

Row 19 Using **B**, knit.

Rows 20 and 21 Using **A**, knit.

Bind off knitwise.

Sew pocket to the left side of the cardigan.

Knit your teddy...

Head

Using light brown yarn, cast on 5 sts.

Row 1 Kfb 4 times, k1. 9 sts.

Row 2 Purl.

Row 3 (Kfb, k1, kfb) 3 times. 15 sts.

Row 4 Purl.

Row 5 Knit.

Row 6 Purl.

Row 7 (Skpo, k1, k2tog) 3 times. 9 sts.

Row 8 Purl.

Row 9 Knit.

Row 10 Purl.

Body

Row 11 (Kfb, k1, kfb) 3 times. 15 sts.

Row 12 Purl.

Row 13 (Kfb, k3, kfb) 3 times. 21sts.

Rows 14 Purl.

Rows 15 Knit.

Repeat rows 14 and 15 twice, then row 14 once more.

Row 20 Purl.

Row 21 (Skpo, k3, k2tog) 3 times. 15 sts.

Row 22 Purl.

Row 23 K6, k2tog, k7. 14 sts.

Leg 1

Row 24 Purl 7 sts. Turn.

Work in st st for 8 rows.

Cut yarn, thread it through sts and pull together.

Leg 2

Rejoin yarn to stitches on needle.

Purl across 7 sts.

Work in st st for 8 rows.

Cut yarn, thread it through sts and pull together.

Arms (make 2)

Using **B**, cast on 7 sts.

Work in st st for 10 rows.

Cut yarn, thread it though sts and pull together.

Ears (make 2)

Using **B**, cast on 3 sts.

Row 1 Kfb, kfb, k1. 5 sts.

Row 2 Purl

Row 3 K2tog, k1, k2tog. 3 sts.

Cut yarn, thread it though sts and pull together.

To finish...

Sew up the back of bear and fill with a small amount of stuffing.

Sew up legs and fill with stuffing.

Sew up arms and fill with stuffing.

Sew arms and legs to body.

Sew ears to head.

Embroider eyes, nose and mouth.

baby's new look

This practical and stylish cardigan will suit any baby. The colour scheme can easily be adapted to give your own personalised touch to this garment. And why not try knitting teddy in a soft and fluffy eyelash yarn – he'll look just grand!

Little boys would look just gorgeous in this dark blue cardigan design, embellished with touches of pale blue and green and complete with it's very own chocolate brown bear. Simply follow the pattern for the Peekaboo Pocket Cardigan and use the yarns suggested below. Or if you have a little girl, why not try knitting the cardigan in pinks and lilacs and including a cream teddy bear.

materials

Brown bear cardigan

Light-weight (DK) wool yarn (113yd/104m per 1¾oz (50g) ball) in the following colours:

A 4 x balls in dark blue

B 1 x ball in shade green

C 1 x ball in shade 2159 Cream

1 x 3½oz (100g) ball of light-weight (DK) acrylic yarn (325yd/298m per ball) in dark brown for bear

happy bunny

Babies and young children will love
to play with this adorable little bunny,
which is full of charm and character. It
is knitted in a very soft grey woollen yarn
so is cuddly and very safe, as all knitted
and embroidered parts made are of soft
material. There are material inserts for the
ears which add texture and decoration,
and the embroidered face gives it the
bunny an endearingly cheerful look. The
fluffy pompom tail is added to the rabbit's
bottom for a cute finishing touch. I've tied
a bow round his neck, but this is optional
and should be removed if it is given to
a young baby.

*Baby will have lots of fun cuddling
up with a new friend and exploring
the texture of its ears.*

DESIGN SECRETS UNRAVELLED...

I wanted to knit a cuddly rabbit that
didn't have too many different parts.
The face, body, legs and feet are all
knitted in one piece with increases
and decreases used to differentiate
between the various parts. The arms
and ears are the only pieces of the
rabbit that need sewing on afterwards.
I chose a grey yarn but you could use
any colour. You could even make a
stripy rabbit. The pompom tail can be
any size you want.

YARN FOCUS

I chose a soft, grey light-weight yarn to
knit the bunny but you could knit it in
a variety of different yarns. You could
make it even softer by using a fluffy
yarn. Using a different thickness of
yarn would alter the size of the rabbit,
so you could knit a much smaller one
by using thin yarn and small needles.
Alternatively you could knit a larger
rabbit using bulky-weight yarn and
large needles.

happy bunny

MEASUREMENTS

11in (28cm) from the tip of his ears to his feet

GATHER TOGETHER...
materials

1 x 1¾oz (50g) balls of light-weight (DK)
extra fine merino/microfibre/cashmere mix yarn
(142yds/130m per ball) in grey

needles and notions

1 pair of size 6 (4mm) knitting needles
Fabric of your choice
Iron-on interfacing
Oddments of yarn in brown

GAUGE

22 sts and 28 rows to 4in (10cm) in st st

*knit note Keep track of which row of the pattern
you need to work next by using a row counter, or
write the row numbers on a piece of paper and
tick them off as you work them.*

The bunny is quite straightforward to knit. It is all knitted in stockinette stitch
to give a smooth appearance. As it is knitted in one piece, it grows in a
three-dimensional way and the increases and decreases give it roundness.
There are only a few seams to sew: down the back of the head, body and
legs and the arm seam. The shaping on the head helps with the positioning
of the embroidered facial features.

Knit your happy bunny...

Head and body

Cast on 9 sts**.**
Row 1 (Kfb, k1) 4 times, k1. 13 sts.
Row 2 and every alt row Purl.
Row 3 (Kfb, k1, kfb) 4 times, k1. 21 sts.
Row 5 (Kfb, k3, kfb) 4 times, k1. 29 sts.
Row 7 (Kfb, k5, kfb) 4 times, k1. 37 sts.
Row 9 (Kfb, k7, kfb) 4 times, k1. 45 sts.
Row 11 (Kfb, k9, kfb) 4 times, k1. 53 sts.
Row 12 Purl.
Work in st st for 12 rows.
Row 25 (K2tog, k9, skpo) 4 times, k1. 45 sts.
Row 26 and every alt row Purl.
Row 27 (K2tog, k7, skpo) 4 times, k1. 37 sts.
Row 29 (K2tog, k5, skpo) 4 times, k1. 29 sts.
Row 31 Knit.
Row 33 (Kfb, k5, kfb) 4 times, k1. 37 sts.
Row 35 (Kfb, k7, kfb) 4 times, k1. 45 sts.
Row 37 (Kfb, k9, kfb) 4 times, k1. 53 sts.
Row 39 (Kfb, k11, kfb) 4 times, k1. 61 sts.
Row 40 Purl.
Work in st st for 24 rows.
Row 65 (K2tog, k11, skpo) 4 times, k1. 53 sts.
Row 66 and every alt row Purl.
Row 67 (K2tog, k9, skpo) 4 times, k1. 45 sts.
Row 69 (K2tog, k7, skpo) 4 times, k1. 37 sts.
Row 70 Purl.

Legs and feet – continuing on the remaining
37 sts.
Row 71 K17, k2tog, k16, k2tog, turn.
Continue on 17 sts for right leg.
Row 72 Purl.
Work in st st for 36 rows.
Row 109 K7, kfb, kfb, k8. 19 sts.

Row 110 and every alt row Purl.
Row 111 K8, kfb, kfb, k9. 21 sts.
Row 113 K9, kfb, kfb, k10. 23 sts.
Row 115 K10, kfb, kfb, k11. 25 sts.
Row 117 K11, kfb, kfb, k12. 27 sts.
Row 119 K2tog, k23, k2tog. 25 sts.
Row 121 K2tog, k9, k3tog, k9, k2tog. 21 sts.
Row 122 Purl.
Bind off.

Rejoin yarn to sts on needle and work left leg in the
same way.

Arms

Cast on 17 sts.
Work in st st for 36 rows.
Row 37 K7, kfb, kfb, k8. 19 sts.
Row 38 and every alt row Purl.
Row 39 K8, kfb, kfb, k9. 21 sts.
Row 41 K9, kfb, kfb, k10. 23 sts.
Row 43 K10, kfb, kfb, k11. 25 sts.
Row 44 (Skpo) 6 times, k1, (k2tog) 6 times. 13 sts.
Row 45 Purl.
Cut yarn and thread through sts.

Ears

Cast on 5 sts.
Row 1 K1, kfb, kfb, k2. 7 sts.
Row 2 and every alt row Purl.
Row 3 K2, kfb, kfb, k3. 9 sts.
Row 5 K3, kfb, kfb, k4. 11 sts.
Row 6 Purl.
Work in st st for 20 rows.
Row 27 K4, k3tog, k4. 9 sts.

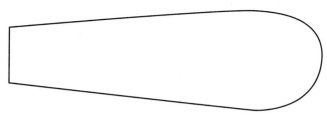

Make sure to choose really soft yarn to make your rabbit even more huggable.

Row 28 Purl.
Row 29 Knit.
Bind off.

To finish...

Body
Fold the body of the rabbit in half with both knit sides together. Sew up from top of head to legs. Turn rabbit the right way out so the knit sides are on the outside. Fill with stuffing.

Legs
Sew from each end leaving a gap of approx 1⅛in (3cm) in the middle. Fill with stuffing and sew up the gap.

Arms
Sew from each end leaving a gap of approx 1⅛in (3cm) in the middle. Fill with stuffing and sew up the gap. Sew on to the body using shaping to position correctly.

Ears
Cut out two fabric ears, line with iron-on interfacing and sew inside the knitted ears. Attach ears to the top of the rabbit's head.

Finishing touches
Make a pompom in cream wool using the template provided. Attach it to the bottom of the rabbit. Embroider nose, eyes and mouth onto the rabbit's face using the shaping to get the correct position.

fun finger puppets

Finger puppets help bring a story to life and are great for young children. I have designed four finger puppets that will appeal to a young child's imagination – a friendly lion, a cheeky cat, a mischievous monkey and a happy hen. Each puppet is knitted using the same basic pattern, which is simply changed by using different coloured and textured yarn. Embroidery and appliqué add the extra detail needed to give the puppets character. Quick to make and full of fun, they are the perfect project for complete beginners.

This mischievous monkey is ready to play and guaranteed to delight your baby.

DESIGN SECRETS UNRAVELLED...

I wanted to make the finger puppets for everyone to knit so I kept my design simple. Each character has a white knitted face so that the embroidered features stand out. The embroidery and appliqué bring the finger puppets to life. They are very quick to knit, so you could make a whole family or farmyard of puppets.

YARN FOCUS

I knitted these finger puppets using a fairly standard light-weight yarn, but you could be really experimental with the yarns you choose and make finger puppets of all different textures. For example, the cat could be knitted in a fluffy angora yarn. For a child's finger you could knit with a finer yarn and smaller needles, creating a baby puppet. You could then make a bigger puppet for the mummy and daddy so you have a family of puppets.

fun finger puppets

MEASUREMENTS
Each puppet is approx 3in (7.5cm) tall

GATHER TOGETHER...
materials
A Less than 1 x 1¾oz (50g) ball of light-weight
(DK) wool/microfibre/cashmere mix yarn in each
of the following colours:
B Face (for all puppets): cream
Friendly lion: orange
Cheeky cat: black
Mischievous monkey: camel
Happy hen: brown

needles and notions
1 pair of size 6 (4mm) knitting needles
Friendly lion: 2 shades of orange felt for mane
Cheeky cat: black felt for ears
Mischievous monkey: camel-coloured felt for
nose and ears
Happy hen: red, orange and brown felt for
comb, beak and tail
Oddments of black, brown, pink and yellow yarn
for features

GAUGE
Gauge is not important for this project

Stockinette stitch is used for all the puppets because this gives a smooth finish that creates the perfect background for adding details. The faces were knitted in the same cream wool using the intarsia technique. Make sure that the yarns are wrapped round one another to avoid making holes.

Knit your finger puppet...

Basic finger puppet pattern
Cast on 16 sts in **A**.
Work in st st for 12 rows.
Row 13 K6 **A**, k4 **B**, k6 **A**.
Row 14 P5 **A**, p6 **B**, p5 **A**.
Row 15 K4 **A**, k8 **B**, k4 **A**.
Row 16 P4 **A**, p8 **B**, p4 **A**.
Row 17 K5 **A**, k6 **B**, k5 **A**.
Row 18 P6 **A**, p4 **B**, p6 **A**.
Row 19 Using **A**, K.
Row 20 (P2tog), rep to end of row. 8 sts.
Row 21 (K2tog), rep to end of row. 4 sts.
Cut yarn and pull it through sts to close.

Sew up back of finger puppet.

Adding detail to each puppet...

Friendly lion
Knit the basic finger puppet pattern using the
orange yarn as **A**.

Tail
Attach a length of orange yarn to the bottom back
of the puppet. Crochet approximately 16 chain sts
and bind off.
Using yellow yarn, create little loops of wool
at the end of the tail. This creates a fluffy effect.
Unravelling some of this yarn also helps to give
a more fluffy appearance.
Mane
Cut out the lion's mane in two shades of orange
felt. Position the mane so that the white face
comes through the hole. Sew one on top of the
other using yellow yarn.
Face
Embroider the nose using pink yarn and the face
features using brown yarn.

Cheeky cat

Knit the basic finger puppet pattern using the black yarn as **A**.

Tail

Attach a length of black wool to the bottom back of the puppet. Crochet approximately 16 chain sts and bind off.

Ears

Cut out two cat's ears in black felt. Sew the ears to the top of the head using the shaping as a guide to position them correctly.

Face

On the white face embroider the nose using pink wool and the face features using brown.

Mischievous monkey

Knit the basic finger puppet pattern using the camel-coloured yarn as **A**.

Tail

Attach a length of camel yarn to the bottom of the back of the puppet. Crochet approximately 16 chain sts and bind off.

Ears

Cut out two monkey's ears in camel-coloured felt. Sew the ears to the top of the head using the shaping as a guide to position them correctly.

Face

Cut out the monkey's nose in the camel-coloured felt and place it on the white face. Embroider the nose and mouth on the felt and the eyes on the white face.

Happy hen

Knit the basic finger puppet pattern using the brown yarn as **A**.

Comb

Cut out the comb in red felt. Sew the comb to the top of the head using the shaping as a guide to position it correctly.

Beak

Cut out the beak in orange felt and attach it in the middle of the white face using two stitches. Embroider the eyes above the beak in brown yarn.

Tail

Cut out two feather tails using two shades of brown felt. Attach them to the back of the bottom of the puppet.

cosy toes warmer

This soft and fluffy cosy toes is designed to keep baby warm and snug during both the day and the night. It is knitted in a soft, fluffy yarn and has a pink seed stitch border which adds colour and interest to the garment. It is buttoned down the front to make it easy to get on and off and it is closed in at the bottom so that your baby's feet are contained. This means that your baby cannot kick it off in their sleep as they would a blanket, guaranteeing a peaceful winter night. The ears sewn to the hood give it a delightfully cute appearance, which you will not be able to resist.

This cosy toes will keep your baby snug and warm even on the coldest winter night.

DESIGN SECRETS UNRAVELLED...

The cosy toes is designed as a warm hooded and armed sleeping bag for baby, but you can leave the bottom open to make a cosy dressing gown for an older child. I knitted the main part in a fluffy yarn and used a fine pink yarn to accentuate the ribs and to add a border decoration to the design. Knitting the two yarns together gives a random mottled effect.

YARN FOCUS

I used a fluffy, cream light-weight yarn to make this piece because it is so soft to touch. For the borders and ribs I added a very thin pink yarn which is knitted with the fluffy yarn. You could use any fine yarn to give the same effect. You could knit the cosy toes using a soft but thick yarn which would give a smoother effect to the garment but would show the stitches more clearly.

cosy toes warmer

MEASUREMENTS
To fit size in months: 3–6
Actual chest measurement: 12½in (32cm)
Bottom to top of shoulders – 18½in (47cm)
Bottom to top of hood – 27½in (70cm)

GATHER TOGETHER...
materials
A 5 x 1oz (25g) balls of light-weight (DK)
100% polyester bouclé yarn (92yd/85m per ball)
in cream
B 1 x 1¾oz (50g) ball of fine (4ply) wool/
polyamide mix yarn (224yd/205m per ball)
in pink

needles and notions
1 pair of size 10 (6mm) and size 10½ (7.5mm)
knitting needles for sleeve cuffs and ears
10 buttons

GAUGE
12 sts and 18 rows to 4in (10cm) in st st using
size 10½ (7.5mm) needles

The cosy toes is knitted mainly in stockinette stitch but the buttonhole borders and border around the hood are knitted in seed stitch. There is a simple rib pattern for the cuffs of the sleeves. When you knit the thick and thin yarns together, make sure you pull the fine yarn tight to form neat edges to the side of the border.

Knit your cosy toes warmer...

Back
Using size 10½ (7.5mm) needles and **A**, cast on 40 sts.
Work in st st for 13¾in (35cm) or required length.
Raglan armholes
Bind off 2 sts at beginning of next 2 rows.
Decrease 1 st each end of every 4th row until 28 sts remain.
Transfer stitches to holder.

Left front
Using size 7.5mm needles and **A**, cast on 25 sts.
Row 1 K20, using **A** and **B** tog k1, p1, k1, p1, k1.
Row 2 Using **A** and **B** tog k1, p1, k1, p1, k1, using **A** only p20.
Row 3 K20, using **A** and **B** tog k1, p1, k1, p1, k1.
Row 4 Using **A** and **B** yarn tog k1, p1, k1, p1, k1, using **A** only p20.
Repeat these rows for 13¾in (35cm) or required length, ending with a purl row.
Raglan armholes (cont with moss stitch border throughout shaping)
Row 1 Bind off 2 sts, k to end of row.
Row 2 Purl.
Row 3 Knit.
Rows 4 and 6 Purl.
Row 5 Knit.
Row 7 K2tog, k to end of row.

Repeat rows 4 to 7 until 17 sts remain.
Purl 1 row.
Transfer stitches to holder.

Right front
Using size 10½ (7.5mm) needles and **A**, cast on 25 sts.
Row 1 Using **A** and **B** tog k1, p1, k1, p1, k1, using **A** only k20.
Row 2 P20, using **A** and **B** tog k1, p1, k1, p1, k1.
Start buttonholes
Row 3 Using **A** and **B** tog k1, p1, yfd, p2tog, k1, using **A** only k20.
Row 4 P20, using **A** and **B** tog k1, p1, k1, p1, k1.
Repeat rows 1 and 2 for 13¾in (35cm) ending with a knit row, adding buttonholes (row 3) every 10 rows.
Raglan armholes (cont with moss stitch border throughout shaping)
Row 1 Bind off 2 sts, p to end of row.
Complete as for left front, reversing shaping and continuing with buttonholes every 10 rows until 17 sts remain.
Purl 1 row.
Transfer stitches to holder.

Knit the cosy toes in a soft bouclé yarn to make a comfortable and cuddly garment for your baby.

Sleeves (make 2)

Using size 10.5 (7.5mm) and **A** and **B** together, cast on 24 sts.

Row 1 (K1, p1), rep to end of row.
Row 2 (K1, p1), rep to end of row.

Repeat row 1 and 2 twice more.
Change to size 10.5 (7.5mm) needles.

Row 7 Using **A** only, Knit.
Row 8 Purl.
Row 9 Inc 1 st at beg and end of row.

Continue in st st increasing each end of every 4th row to 40 sts.
Purl 1 row.

Raglan shaping

Bind off 2 sts at beg of next 2 rows.
K2tog each end of every other row to 12 sts.
Purl 1 row.
Transfer stitches to holder

To finish...

With RS facing, put saved stitches onto a circular needle for flexibility as follows: 17 sts from left side, 12 sts from left sleeve, 22 sts from back, 12 sts from right sleeve, 17 sts from right side.
Sew the raglan sleeve to the front and back armholes and then down the arm seams and the side seams. (This is best done by having right sides together and carefully backstitching the pieces together.)
Starting from the knit side and making sure you continue to work buttonholes every 10 rows):

Row 1 Using **A** and **B** tog, k1, p1, k1, p1, k1, using **A** only, k11, k2tog, k10, k2tog, k20, k2tog, k10, k2tog, k11, using **A** and **B** tog, k1, p1, k1, p1, k1.
Cont adding **B** to the border.

Row 2 Using **A** and **B** tog, k1, p1, k1, p1, k1, using **A** only, p66, using **A** and **B** tog, k1, p1, k1, p1, k1.

Neck shaping

Row 3 Using **A** and **B** tog, k1, p1, k1, p1, k1, using **A** only, k9, skpo, k2tog, k7, skpo, k2tog, k2, skpo, k2, skpo, k2, k2tog, k2, k2tog, k2, skpo, k2tog, k7, skpo, k2tog, k9, using DK and 4 ply yarn tog, k1, p1, k1, p1, k1.

Row 4 Using **A** and **B** tog, k1, p1, k1, p1, k1, using **A** only, p54, using **A** and **B** tog, k1, p1, k1, p1, k1.

Row 5 Bind off 5 sts, using **A** and **B** tog p1, k1, using **A** only k52, k1, p1, k1, p1, k1

Row 6 Bind off 5 sts purlwise, using **A** and **B** tog p1, k1, using **A** only p48, k1, p1, k1.

Cont adding **B** to the border.

Row 7 K1, p1, k1, k48, k1, p1, k1.

Work in st st for 8in (20cm).

Next row K1, p1, k1, k18, (k3tog) 4 times, k18, k1, p1, k1.

Next row Purl.

Bind off.

Ears (make 2)

Using 6mm needles and **A** and **B** tog, cast on 5 sts.

Row 1 K1, kfb, kfb, k2. 7 sts.

Row 2 and every alt row Purl.

Row 3 K2, kfb, kfb, k3. 9 sts.

Row 5 K3, kfb, kfb, k4. 11 sts.

Row 7 K4, kfb, kfb, k5. 13 sts.

Row 9 K5, kfb, kfb, k6. 15 sts.

Row 11 Knit.

Row 12 Purl.

Bind off.

To finish...

Sew in ends.

With right sides facing sew up top of hood using back stitch.

Sew buttons on to border.

Sew ears onto hood positioning them either side of the seam.

baby's new look

This is a great project to use to experiment with combining different thicknesses of yarn in the border sections. If you want to use this as a sleeping bag, make sure the yarn used for the main part of the Cosy Toes is soft enough for baby's delicate skin.

Here, I have experimented with two different colourways, perfect for the autumn and winter months when the nights get colder and your baby will really benefit from the warmth of a sleeping bag. For the autumn design, I have created a tweed effect by combining yarns in two colours for a unique look. They would look great on a boy and you can experiment by adding different buttons to get the look you want.

Materials
Winter blues
A 5 x 1¾oz (50g) balls of light-weight (DK) cotton/acrylic mix yarn (175yd/160m per ball) in grey
B 1 x 1¾oz (50g) balls of fine (4ply) nylon/acrylic mix yarn (247yd/226m per ball) in pale blue
Autumn tweed
A 2 x 1¾oz (50g) balls of light-weight (DK) wool/acrylic mix yarn (120yd/110m per ball) in grey mixed with **B** 3 1¾oz (50g) balls of fine (4ply) wool/nylon mix yarn (224yd/205m per ball) in lilac
C 1 x 1¾oz (50g) ball of light-weight (DK) Bamboo/Wool mix yarn (104yd/ 95m per ball) in maroon

cute chicken mobile

This adorable little chicken has real character. It is made using cream and brown woollen yarn in textured stripes and as it is knitted primarily in stockinette stitch, it is surprisingly easy to make. You could keep to natural colours as here, or why not try knitting the chicken with multicoloured yarns for a bold variation that will really brighten up your baby's nursery. The chicken can be knitted as an individual toy or used in a mobile, with accompanying little pompom chicks (see page 89). When the mobile is hung above the cot, it will keep your baby entertained for hours.

Your baby will be delighted by the chicken's character and charm, whether it is hanging from a mobile or as an individual toy.

DESIGN SECRETS UNRAVELLED...

The head and body of the chicken is knitted in one piece with increases and decreases separating the two parts. The wings are knitted and sewn on afterwards and the legs are made from crocheting a chain from the yarn left over from knitting the feet.

I chose cream and brown yarns and used a basic stockinette stitch but added ridged textures by knitting instead of purling rows. I used felt for the chicken's tail and crown but you could use other fabrics to give different effects. If you use a fabric that might fray, make sure you use some iron-on interfacing to keep the edges neat.

YARN FOCUS

I chose soft, cream and brown light-weight yarn to knit the chicken, but you could experiment with a variety of different yarns such as soft cotton or a fluffy yarn. You could also vary the size of the hen by using thick or thin yarns. Because making the hen requires only small amounts of yarn, you could knit it from ends that you have left over from other knitting projects.

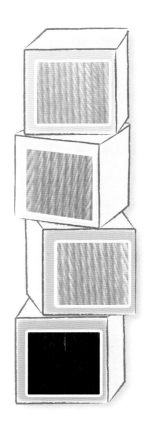

cute chicken mobile

MEASUREMENTS

Top of head to bottom of feet – 12in (30cm)

GATHER TOGETHER...
materials

1 x 1¾oz (50g) balls of extra fine merino/acrylic
microfibre/cashmere mix yarn (142yd/130m per
ball) in each of **A** cream and **B** brown
C 1 x 1¾oz (50g) ball of light-weight (DK)
superwash wool (137yd/125m per ball) in yellow

needles and notions

1 pair of size 6 (4mm) knitting needles
Red and brown felt for crown and tail
Stuffing

GAUGE

22 sts and 30 rows to 4in (10cm)

The hen is primarily knitted in stockinette stitch to give a smooth appearance but with texture added by knit structure and pattern. There are only a few seams to sew up once you have finished knitting. If you leave a reasonable length of yarn when you cast on, it can be used to sew up seams at the end of the project. The increases and decreases on the head help with the positioning of the embroidered facial features, beak and crown.

Knit your chicken...

Body

Using **A**, cast on 9 sts.
Row 1 (Kfb, k1), rep to last st, k1. 13 sts.
Row 2 and every alt row Purl.
Row 3 (Kfb, k1, kfb), rep to last st, k1. 21 sts.
Row 5 (Kfb, k3, kfb), rep to last st, k1. 29 sts.
Row 7 (Kfb, k5, kfb), rep to last st, k1. 37 sts.
Row 9 (Kfb, k7, kfb), rep to last st, k1. 45 sts.
Row 10 Purl.
Work in st st for 12 rows.
Row 23 (K2tog, k7, skpo) 4 times, k1. 37 sts.
Row 24 Purl.
Change to **B**.
Row 25 Knit.
Row 26 Purl.
Row 27 (K1**B**, k3**A**), rep to last stitch, k1**B**.
Row 28 P2**B**, (p1**A**, p3**B**), rep to last 3 sts, p1**A**, p2**B**.
Row 29 Using **B**, knit.
Row 30 Purl.
Change to **A**.
Row 31 (Kfb, k7, kfb), rep to last st, k1. 45 sts.
Row 32 Purl.
Repeat rows 25 to 30.
Change to **A**.
Row 39 (Kfb, k9, kfb), rep to last st, k1. 53 sts.
Row 40 Purl.
Repeat rows 25 to 30.
Change to **A**.
Row 47 (Kfb, k11, kfb), rep to last st, k1. 61 sts.
Row 48 Purl.
Repeat rows 25 to 30.
Change to **A**.
Row 55 (Kfb, k13, kfb), rep to last st, k1. 69 sts.

Row 56 Purl.
Repeat rows 25 to 30.
Continue in **B**.
Row 63 (K1, k3tog), rep to last stitch, k1. 35 sts.
Row 64 Purl.
Row 65 K1, (k3 tog), rep to last st, k1. 13 sts.
Row 66 Purl.
Cut yarn and thread through sts.

Wings

Using **B**, cast on 3 sts.
Row 1 Kfb, kfb, k1. 5 sts.
Row 2 and every alt row Purl.
Row 3 K1, kfb, kfb, k2. 7 sts.
Row 5 K2, kfb, kfb, k3. 9 sts.
Row 7 K3, kfb, kfb, k4. 11 sts.
Row 9 K4, kfb, kfb, k5. 13 sts.
Row 11 K5, kfb, kfb, k6. 15 sts.
Row 12 Purl.
Work in st st for 12 rows.
Row 25 K5, skpo, k1, k2tog, k5. 13 sts.
Row 26 Purl.
Bind off.

Beak

Using **C**, cast on 3 sts.
Row 1 Kfb, kfb, k1. 5 sts.
Row 2 and every alt row Purl.
Row 3 K1, kfb, kfb, k2. 7 sts.
Row 5 K2, kfb, kfb, k3. 9 sts.
Row 7 K3, kfb, kfb, k4. 11 sts.
Row 8 Purl.
Bind off.

Feet (make 2)

Using **C**, cast on 3 sts leaving a long piece of yarn which will be used to crochet the legs.

Row 1 Kfb, kfb, k1. 5 sts.

Row 2 and every alt row Purl.

Row 3 K1, kfb, kfb, k2. 7 sts.

Row 5 K2, kfb, kfb, k3. 9 sts.

Row 7 K3, kfb, kfb, k4. 11 sts.

Row 9 K4, kfb, kfb, k5. 13 sts.

Row 11 K4, skpo, k1, k2tog, k4. 11 sts.

Row 13 K3, skpo, k1, k2tog, k3. 9 sts.

Row 15 K2, skpo, k1, k2tog, k2. 7 sts.

Row 17 K1, skpo, k1, k2tog, k1. 5 sts.

Row 18 P5tog.

Cut off yarn leaving a length of approx 12in (30cm) to crochet later.

To finish...

Body

Sew up from the top of the head to the base of the body leaving a small gap to put the stuffing in. Fill with stuffing and close gap.

Wings

Stitch the wings to each side of the bird's body using the patterns on the body to position them correctly.

Beak

Fold beak in half and sew down the seam. Fill with a small amount of stuffing, Stitch the beak to the bird's head using the shaping at the front of the head to position it correctly.

Legs and feet

Fold the feet in half and make a crochet stitch through both sides using the leftover yarn. Crochet a chain of 12 rows from the leftover yarn attached to the feet. Sew round the edges of the feet. Sew the crochet chain with the foot on the end on to the base of the body.

Tail

Cut out three feathers using the template in three different coloured felts. Sew the bottom of the feathers to the back of the bird.

To finish...

Cut out the red crown and sew it to the top of the head, bending it around to fit properly. Embroider eyes each side of the head using brown yarn (use the picture as a guide).

Make your mobile...

To make the mobile, attach a length of wool to the top of each bird. The chicks have a little yarn loop (created when making them) which can be used to attach the yarn. For the chicken, you will need to thread one end of the wool through the top of the head with a needle. Knot this securely.

You can hang these birds to anything. If you want to create a more traditional looking mobile, I would suggest crossing over two small pieces of wood and attaching the hen and chicks to each side so that they hang down to your desired length.

Make your chicks...

Using the template cut out two pieces of card. Place the two circles of card on top of each other and wrap the yellow yarn in and out of the centre hole while working your way around the pompom ring. Continue wrapping the wool around the ring until it nearly touches in the middle.

Carefully cut around the edge of the pompom, slipping your scissors between the two rings. This makes the cutting easier.

Pull the two pieces of card slightly apart and tie string or wool around the pompom centre. Knot tightly and leave about 8in (20cm) of yarn hanging below the pompom to use later for the legs. Tie another piece of yarn around the pompom middle and leave another end of 8in (20cm). You should have four pieces of hanging yarn. Remove the cardboard rings.

Knot two strands together for roughly 1⅛in (3cm) below the pompom. Repeat for the second leg. Cut out the feet in felt and sew on to the bottom of each knotted leg.

For the face, cut out the beak, fold it in half and sew it to the centre of the pompom. Cut out two eyes in white felt. Embroider a brown stitch to the middle of each eye and glue it above the beak.

beautiful blanket

This soft blanket is knitted in chunky cream yarn using different stitches to create texture and pattern. The blocks of pattern give the impression of an heirloom patchwork quilt, without all the hassle of sewing up the patches. It can be used to wrap up baby or as a cosy cot blanket and would make a delightful gift to welcome a new arrival. Choose a soft yarn to keep baby warm and comfortable. I chose cream, which is a lovely neutral shade, however you could substitute this for pink for a girl, blue for a boy, or even a multi-coloured design with each square being a different colour, as well as texture, for baby to explore.

Use a machine-washable yarn to make this blanket practical as well as pretty.

DESIGN SECRETS UNRAVELLED...

The blanket is designed using seed stitch borders to enclose textured patterns created by the different stitches used. The smooth stockinette stitch contrasts with the bumpy purl stitch and the bobble effect of bramble stitch. You could easily simplify the design by just using grids of stockinette stitch, garter stitch and purl stitch. I only used one colour for the design but you could work the squares in different colours or add interest by usinf a coloured yarn for the seed stitch border.

YARN FOCUS

The blanket is knitted in a plain bulky-weight yarn. Even though there are a lot of stitches, this bulky-weight yarn knits up quite quickly. I chose a cream yarn to make it suitable for both boys and girls. However, you could use any yarn in any colour to knit this blanket. If you used a finer yarn and smaller needles, you could increase the number of rows of squares to make sure the blanket is still the right size.

beautiful blanket

MEASUREMENTS
33⅜in (85cm) long x 27½in (70cm) wide

GATHER TOGETHER...
materials
5 x 3½oz (100g) balls of bulky (chunky)
acrylic/cotton/wool mix yarn
(171yd/156m per ball) in cream

needles and notions
1 pair of size 10½ (7mm) knitting needles

GAUGE
14 sts and 19 rows to 4in (10cm) over pattern sts

I have drawn out a grid for reference when knitting the blanket. This makes it easier to follow the textured pattern. The outside border is made up of 5 seed stitches by 5 rows, the textured squares are made up of 14 stitches by 19 rows and the borders between the squares are made up of 3 seed stitches. Once you get used to using the grid, you can enjoy watching the design grow and the pattern taking shape.

Knit your blanket...

Cast on 92 sts.
Row 1 (K1, p1), rep to end of row.
Row 2 (P1, k1), rep to end of row.
Repeat these 2 rows once and then row 1 once more.
Row 6 P1, k1, p1, k1, p1 (border), k14 (st st square), k1, p1, k1 (border), p14 (purl square), p1, k1, p1 (border), p14 (bramble stitch square), k1, p1, k1 (border), p14 (purl square), p1, k1, p1 (border), k14 (st st square), k1, p1, k1, p1, k1 (border).
Row 7 K1, p1, k1, p1, k1, p14, p1, k1, p1, p14, k1, p1, k1, k1, *(k1, p1, k1) in next st, p3tog, repeat from * 3 times, k1, p1, k1, p1, p14, k1, p1, k1, p14, p1, k1, p1, k1, p1.
Row 8 As row 6.
Row 9 K1, p1, k1, p1, k1, p14, p1, k1, p1, p14, k1, p1, k1, k1, *p3tog, (k1, p1, k1) in next st, rep from * 3 times, k1, p1, k1, p1, p14, k1, p1, k1, p14, p1, k1, p1, k1, p1.
Rows 10 to 21 Repeat rows 6 to 9 three times.
Row 22 As row 6.
Row 23 As row 7.
Row 24 As row 8.
Row 25 (K1, p1), rep to end of row.
Row 26 (P1, k1), rep to end of row.
Repeat rows 25 and 26 once and then row 25 once more.

Row 30 P1, k1, p1, k1, p1, k14, k1, p1, k1, p14, p1, k1, p1, k14, k1, p1, k1, p14, p1, k1, p1, k14, k1, p1, k1, p1, k1.
Row 31 K1, p1, k1, p1, k1, p14, p1, k1, p1, k1, *(k1, p1, k1) in next st, p3tog, repeat from * 3 times, k1, k1, p1, k1, p14, p1, k1, p1, k1, *(k1, p1, k1) in next st,

p3tog, rep from * 3 times, k1, k1, p1, k1, p14, p1, k1, p1, k1, p1.
Row 32 As row 30.
Row 33 K1, p1, k1, p1, k1, p14, p1, k1, p1, k1, *p3tog, (k1, p1, k1) in next st, rep from * 3 times, k1, k1, p1, k1, p14, p1, k1, p1, k1, *p3tog, (k1, p1, k1) in next st, rep from * 3 times, k1, k1, p1, k1, p14, p1, k1, p1, k1, p1.
Rows 34 to 45 Repeat rows 30 to 33 three times.
Row 46 As row 30.
Row 47 As row 31.
Row 48 As row 32.
Row 49 (K1, p1), rep to end of row.
Row 50 (P1, k1), rep to end of row.
Repeat these two rows once and then row 49 once more.

Row 54 P1, k1, p1, k1, p1, p14, k1, p1, k1, k14, p1, k1, p1, p14, k1, p1, k1, p14, p1, k1, p1, k1, k14, k1, p1, k1, p1, k1.
Row 55 K1, p1, k1, p1, k1, k1, *(k1, p1, k1) in next st, p3tog, rep from * 3 times, k1, p1, k1, p1, p14, k1, p1, k1, p14, p1, k1, p1, k14, k1, p1, k1, k1, *(k1, p1, k1) in next st, p3tog, rep from * 3 times, k1, p1, k1, p1, k1, p1.
Row 56 As row 54.
Row 57 K1, p1, k1, p1, k1, k1, *p3tog (k1, p1, k1) in next st, rep from * 3 times, k1, p1, k1, p1, p14, k1, p1, k1, p14, p1, k1, p1, p14, k1, p1, k1, k1, *p3tog (k1, p1, k1) in next st, rep from * 3 times, k1, p1, k1, p1, k1, p1.
Rows 58 to 45 Repeat rows 54 to 57 three times.
Row 70 As row 54.
Row 71 As row 55.
Row 72 As row 56.
Row 73 (K1, p1), rep to end of row.
Row 74 (P1, k1), rep to end of row.
Repeat these two rows once and then row 73 once.

Rows 78 to 101 Repeat rows 6 to 29.
Rows 102 to 125 Repeat rows 54 to 77.
Rows 126 to 149 Repeat rows 30 to 53.
Rows 150 to 173 repeat rows 6 to 29.
Bind off.

To finish...
Weave in yarn ends.

Key

P	All rows purl.
St st	Stockinette stitch – 1 row knit, 1 row purl.
Br	Bramble stitch: **Rows 1 and 3** Purl. **Row 2** K1, *(k1, p1, k1) into next st, p3tog, rep from * 3 times, k1. **Row 4** K1, *(p3tog, k1, p1, k1) into next st, rep from * 3 times, k1. Repeat rows 1 to 4.
Seed st	**Row 1** (K1, p1), rep to end of row. **Row 2** (P1, k1), rep to end of row. Repeat rows 1 and 2.

St St		P		Br		P		St St
P		Br		St St		Br		P
Br		St St		P		St St		Br
St St		P		Br		P		St St
Br		St St		P		St St		Br
P		Br		St St		Br		P
St St		P		Br		P		St St

5 stitches moss stitch

3 stitches moss stitch

baby's new look

This blanket would look equally good in more than one colour. Why not create a traditional patchwork quilt effect by using several different colours? That way it is easy to match the colour scheme in your nursery. Use a finer yarn and smaller needles to make a summer weight blanket.

With these three different swatches it is clear to see the diversity of textures and patterns that can be achieved by using a variety of types of yarns and stitches for the squares that make up the design. These three swatches would go together well to create a warm and snuggly blanket with a modern look and autumnal feel.

materials

Tweed stocking stitch sample

1¾oz (50g) balls of light-weight (DK) wool/acrylic mix yarn wool (120yd/110m per ball) in blue knitted with 1¾oz (50g) balls of fine (4 ply) wool/polyamide mix yarn (224yd/205m per ball) in mauve.

Pale tweed bramble sample

1¾oz (50g) balls of fine (4 ply) wool/polyamide mix yarn (224yd/205m per ball) in:

A 2 strands of pink

B 1 strand of grey

C 1 strand of light blue

Blue moss stitch sample

14oz (400g) balls of acrylic/wool mix yarn (920yd/840m per ball) in blue

funky floral
pyjama bag

Children will love this brightly coloured
pyjama bag. It is knitted with a circular
needle so it has no side seams, to ensure
a flawless finish. The pattern is knitted
using a Fair Isle method (see page
114) and runs colourfully around the
bag. Although it is perfect for storing a
favourite pair of pyjamas, the bag can
have other uses. It can be made larger
or smaller by adding or taking away
extra rows and lines of squares and if
you wanted, you could turn the bag into
a hot water bottle cover, a shoe bag or
even a little bag to keep baby's toys.

*Use acrylic or cotton yarns for their
strength and ease of care.*

DESIGN SECRETS UNRAVELLED...

I started this bag from the grass at
the bottom and worked up to the sky
at the top using a circular needle so
that the bag is seamless. The colours
in the pattern are worked out using a
square grid. Each little square on the
grid represents one stitch. The flower
design is made up of 20 squares
horizontally and 30 squares vertically.
This is repeated four times. You can
easily alter the colours in the pattern.
For example, instead of only using red
yarn for the flowers, use a variety of
colours such as pink, orange, mauve
and white. You can even change the
position of the leaves and petals by
altering the grid.

YARN FOCUS

I chose a light-weight yarn but knitted
with two strands as I wanted a dense
structure for the bag. You could knit
the bag in a thicker yarn but be careful
not to use too thick a yarn as the
loops made by the Fair Isle method
of introducing colour can make the
structure quite bulky. Using a thinner
yarn would mean that the flowers
were smaller, so it would probably be
necessary to add another 20 stitches
and more rows for the grass and sky.

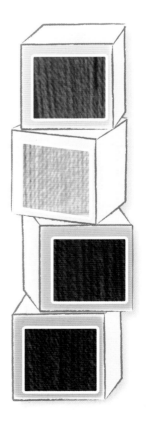

funky floral pyjama bag

MEASUREMENTS

12in (30cm) long and 18in (46cm) in circumference

GATHER TOGETHER...
materials

1 x 3½oz (100g) balls of light-weight (DK) 100% acrylic yarn (325yd/298m per ball) in each of **A** green, **B** blue and **C** red. Small amount of yarn in colour **D** yellow.

needles and notions

1 32in (80cm) long size 8 (5mm) circular knitting needle
Small crochet hook

GAUGE

19 sts and 24 rows to 4in (10cm)

The pyjama bag is knitted in the round using a circular needle so every row is a knit row. The pattern is more challenging to make due to the Fair Isle technique used. The flower design is shown on the chart which indicates the colours to use and number of stitches to be worked. Make sure you link the different colours of yarn carefully around one another to avoid large loops of yarn on the inside of the bag. I wound the threads round each other every three stitches, to ensure that the inside of the bag is very neat. When knitting the pattern, be careful to keep the threads you are carrying across the back of the fabric loose so that the bag keeps its shape.

This fun bag featuring bold, bright flowers is sure to brighten up any nursery.

Knit your pyjama bag...

Using **A**, cast on 80 sts.
Knit 12 rounds in **A** then start the pattern on the chart. There are 40 sts on the chart, so you need to repeat it twice.
After working the 30 rows of the pattern, knit 12 rows in **B**.

Eyelet holes for tie

Round 1 Purl.
Round 2 Knit.
Round 3 Knit.
Round 4 (K2, yfd, k2tog), repeat to end of round.
Round 5 Knit.
Round 6 Knit.
Round 7 Purl.
Rounds 8 to 18 Knit.
Bind off.

Ties (make 2)

Using 2 strands of **C** and chain stitch, crochet a chain 31⅞in (80cm) long.

To finish...

Sew in all loose threads.
Neatly sew up the bottom of bag.
Gently iron the top of the bag so it is flat.
Starting from the side, thread one of the ties through the eyelet holes. Starting from the other side, thread the second tie through the eyelet holes.
Tie knots in the ends of the ties.
The bag can be drawn up by pulling the ties.

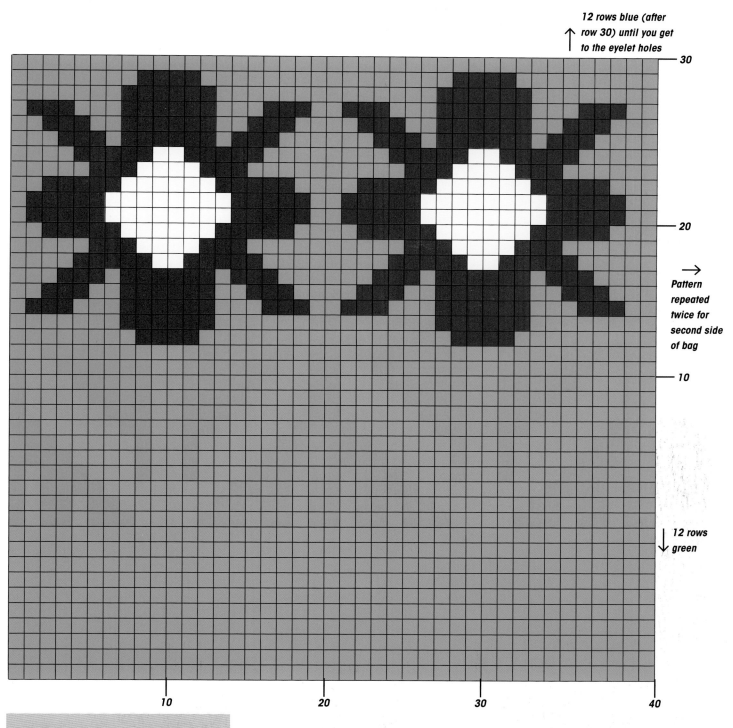

12 rows blue (after row 30) until you get to the eyelet holes

30

20

→

Pattern repeated twice for second side of bag

10

12 rows green

10   20   30   40

Notes:
1. Work 12 rows in **A** before starting the chart.
2. Work 12 rows in **B** after finishing the chart before working the eyelet holes.
3. The pattern is repeated on each side of the bag.

it's all in
the detail...

casting on

Most knitters have their own favoured method for casting on, so I have not specified which method to use. Make sure you do not cast on too tightly. If you do, the edge will not stretch sufficiently and may break. Try using a size larger needle to make sure it is loose enough. Remember to change back to the correct size needle to begin knitting.

CABLE CAST-ON

This method of casting on is used to make a firm edge and needs two needles. To cast on at the beginning of a project, make a slip knot about 6in (15cm) from the end of the yarn and slip it on to a needle held in your left hand.

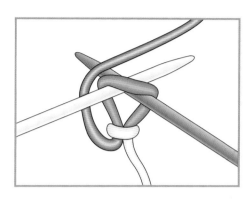

1 Insert the right-hand needle into the slip knot as though to knit it and wrap the yarn around the tip.

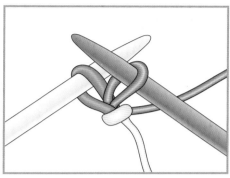

2 Pull a new loop through but do not slip the stitch off the left-hand needle.

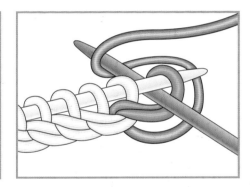

3 Place the loop on to the left-hand needle by inserting the left-hand needle into the front of the loop from right to left.

4 Insert the right-hand needle between the two stitches and wrap the yarn around the tip. When the new loop is pulled through between the stitches, place it on the left-hand needle, as shown in step 3.

Repeat step 4 until you have cast on the required number of stitches.

Extra stitches

To cast on the extra stitches needed in the middle of knitting, work step 4 only, working the first stitch between the next two stitches already on the left-hand needle.

knit stitch

The knit stitch is the classic knitting stitch, and the one that all beginners learn first. It is very versatile when used on its own. Once you have got to grips with this stitch, you can start knitting items in garter stitch.

GARTER STITCH

When you knit each row, the fabric you make is called garter stitch (g st). This has rows of raised ridges on the front and back of the fabric. Garter stitch lies flat, is quite a thick fabric and does not curl at the edges. Garter stitch is ideal for a project that has lots of texture – any fancier stitches would simply be lost. It's also useful for items that are reversible, as it looks the same from both sides.

MAKING THE KNIT STITCH – ENGLISH METHOD

Each knit stitch is made up of four easy steps. The yarn is held at the back of the work (the side facing away from you).

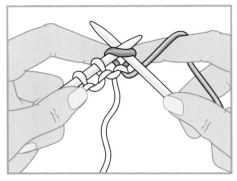

1 Hold the needle with the cast-on stitches in your left hand, and insert the right-hand needle into the front of the stitch from left to right.

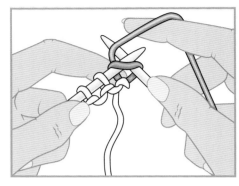

2 Pass the yarn under and around the right-hand needle.

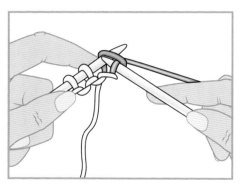

3 Pull the new loop on the right-hand needle through the stitch on the left-hand needle.

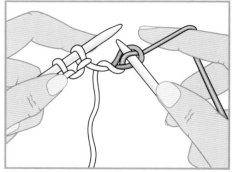

4 Slip the stitch off the left-hand needle. One knit stitch is completed.

Repeat these four steps for each stitch on the left-hand needle. All the stitches on the left-hand needle will be transferred to the right-hand needle, where the new row is formed. At the end of the row, swap the needle with the stitches into your left hand and the empty needle into your right hand to begin the next row.

MAKING THE KNIT STITCH — CONTINENTAL METHOD

In this method the right-hand needle moves to catch the yarn; the yarn is held at the back of the work (the side facing away from you) and is released by the index finger of the left hand. This knit stitch is made up of four steps.

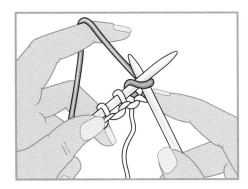

1 Hold the needle with the cast-on stitches in your left hand and the yarn over your left index finger. Insert the right-hand needle into the front of the stitch from left to right.

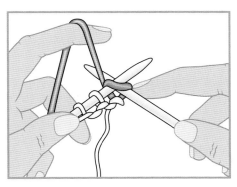

2 Move the right-hand needle down and across the back of the yarn.

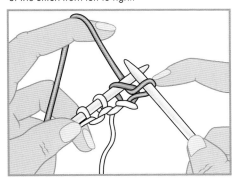

3 Pull the new loop on the right-hand needle through the stitch on the left-hand needle, using the right index finger to hold the new loop if needed.

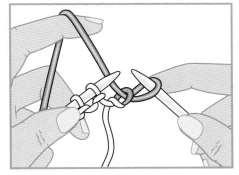

4 Slip the stitch off the left-hand needle. One knit stitch is completed.

Repeat these four steps for each stitch on the left-hand needle. All the stitches on the left-hand needle will be transferred to the right-hand needle where the new row is formed. At the end of the row, swap the needle with the stitches into your left hand and the empty needle into your right hand, and work the next row in the same way.

purl stitch

Purl stitch is the other classic knitting stitch. Once you know both the knit and purl stitches, you can pretty much make anything. One row of knit and one row of purl makes stockinette stitch, which, with its clearly distinguishable right and wrong side, forms the fundamental knitted fabric.

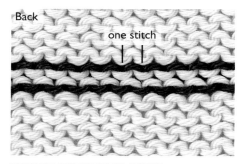

Front

one row

one stitch

STOCKINETTE STITCH

Stockinette stitch (st st) is formed by knitting one row, purling the next row, and then repeating these two rows.

In the knitting instructions for the projects, stockinette stitch is written as follows:

Row 1 (RS) Knit.

Row 2 Purl.

Or, the instructions may be:

Work in st st (1 row k, 1 row p), beg with a k row.

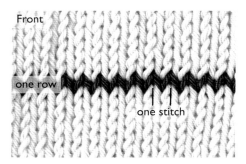

Back

one stitch

REVERSE STOCKINETTE STITCH

Reverse stockinette stitch (rev st st) is when the back of stockinette stitch fabric is used as the right side. This is commonly used as the background for cables, but can also be used as the right side of fabrics knitted in fancy yarns, such as faux fur or fashion yarns. This is because most of the textured effect of the yarn remains on the reverse side of the fabric.

MAKING THE PURL STITCH – ENGLISH METHOD

Each purl stitch is made up of four easy steps. The yarn is held at the front of the work (the side facing you).

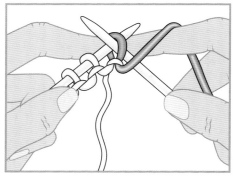

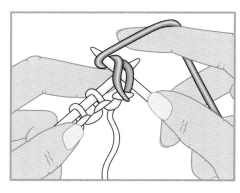

1 Hold the needle with the cast-on stitches in your left hand, and insert the right-hand needle into the front of the stitch from right to left.

2 Pass the yarn over and around the right-hand needle.

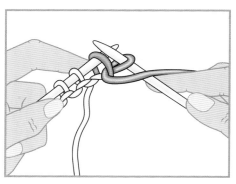

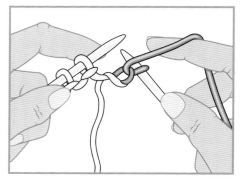

3 Pull the new loop on the right-hand needle through the stitch on the left-hand needle.

4 Slip the stitch off the left-hand needle. One stitch is completed.

Repeat these four steps for each stitch on the left-hand needle. All the stitches on the left-hand needle will be transferred to the right-hand needle, where the new purl row is formed. At the end of the row, swap the needle with the stitches into your left hand and the empty needle into your right hand to begin the next row.

MAKING THE PURL STITCH – CONTINENTAL METHOD

In this method, you can use your index finger to help keep the yarn taut and to hold the new loop formed. This purl stitch is made up of four steps:

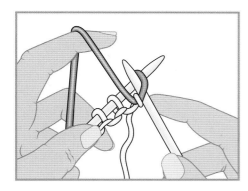

1 Hold the needle with the cast-on stitches in your left hand, and insert the right-hand needle into the front of the stitch from right to left, keeping the yarn at the front of the work.

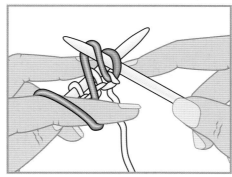

2 Move the right-hand needle from right to left behind the yarn and then from left to right in front of the yarn. Pull your left index finger down in front of the work to keep the yarn taut.

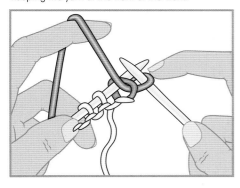

3 Pull the new loop on the right-hand needle through the stitch on the left-hand needle, using the right index finger to hold the new loop if needed.

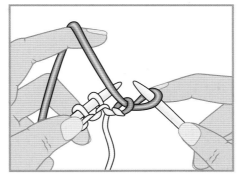

4 Slip the stitch off the left-hand needle. Return the left index finger to its position above the needle. One stitch is completed.

Repeat these four steps for each stitch on the left-hand needle. All the stitches on the left-hand needle will be transferred to the right-hand needle where the new purl row is formed. At the end of the row, swap the needle with the stitches into your left hand and the empty needle into your right hand, and work the next row in the same way.

binding off

Unless specifically instructed to do otherwise, you should bind off in pattern – for example, bind off knitwise on the right side of a piece knitted in stockinette stitch. The various methods are explained below. The bound-off edge should not be too tight otherwise it will pull the knitted fabric in. This is important when binding off a visible edge. If you do tend to bind off tightly, try using a needle a size larger than that used for the knitted fabric.

BIND OFF KNITWISE

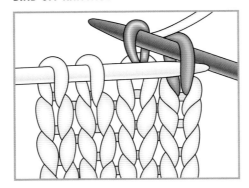

1 Knit two stitches, and insert the tip of the left-hand needle into the front of the first stitch on the right-hand needle.

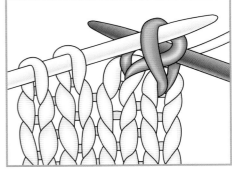

2 Lift this stitch over the second stitch and off the needle.

KNIT PERFECT

When you wish to stop knitting, but aren't ready to bind off yet, always finish the complete row. Finishing in the middle of a row will stretch the stitches and they may slide off the needle. If you need to put your knitting aside for several weeks or even months and do not have time to finish the piece beforehand, mark on the pattern or make a note of where you have got to. If you are working in a regular pattern such as stockinette stitch, when restarting again it is worth unravelling a couple of rows and reknitting them, as stitches left over time on the needles can become stretched and leave an unsightly ridge where you stopped.

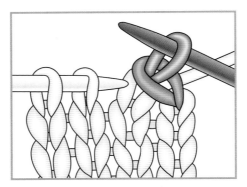

3 One stitch is left on the right-hand needle.

4 Knit the next stitch and lift the second stitch over this and off the needle. Continue in this way until one stitch remains on the right-hand needle.
   Cut the yarn (leaving a length long enough to sew in), thread the end through the last stitch and slip it off the needle. Pull the yarn end to tighten the stitch.

BIND OFF PURLWISE

To bind off on a purl row, simply purl the stitches instead of knitting them.

BIND OFF IN PATTERN

To bind off in rib, you must knit the knit stitches and purl the purl stitches of the rib. If you are working a pattern of cable stitches, you bind off in pattern; once again, you should knit the knit stitches and purl the purl stitches.

knitting in the round

Circular knitting means that the knitted fabric is worked in rounds instead of rows; when you reach the end of a round you simply begin the next without turning the needles. You need different needles from those you usually use for knitting; a circular needle is used to knit the Funky Floral Pyjama Bag (see pages 96–100), but you can also use a set of five double-pointed needles.

You can change onto a circular needle when the stitches become too many to keep safely on the double-pointed needles and also to knit a tube of fabric with no seams. A circular needle is a length of flexible nylon wire fixed between two short needles. Such needles come in several lengths. By knitting in rounds, you produce a fabric with no seams.

DOUBLE-POINTED NEEDLES

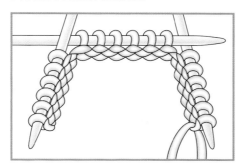

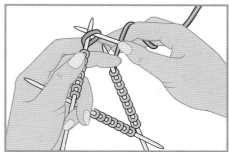

These are available in sets of five: four needles to hold the stitches and one to knit with.

Cast on the required number of stitches onto one needle and then slip them onto the other three so that each has the same number. Arrange the needles into a square, making sure the cast-on edge faces inwards and is not twisted. With the free needle, knit the first cast-on stitch, pulling the yarn up tightly to join the last cast-on stitch with the first. Continue to knit all the stitches off the first needle. You now have a different free needle. Use this to knit the stitches off the second needle. Repeat for the remaining two needles until you reach the end of the round. Place a stitch marker one stitch in from the last stitch so it doesn't fall off the needle.

CIRCULAR NEEDLES

To use a circular needle to knit in rounds, you pick up or cast on the required number of stitches using one of the needle ends. Spread them evenly around the needle, making sure that the stitches face inwards and are not twisted. The stitches should lie closely together and not be pulled too far apart. If the stitches are stretched when the needles are joined, you will need to use a shorter needle.

To identify the beginning of the round, place a marker between the last and first cast-on stitch and slip this on every round. Bring the two needles together and knit the first stitch, pulling up the yarn to prevent a gap. Continue knitting each stitch to reach the marker. One round has been completed. Begin the next round by slipping the marker.

I have also recommended using circular needles for knitting the edgings to some of the garments worked in flat knitting. This is because the circular needle is more flexible and makes it easier to pick up the stitches around the edges. Also, if there are a large number of stitches, these can be accommodated on the wire and the weight of the fabric is held in front of you, on your lap, rather than at the end of long straight needles. Use the circular needle just as you would straight needles; turn at the end of every row.

increasing stitches

Many of the projects in this book call for some shaping – otherwise all the items you ever knit would be square or rectangular. There are several ways to increase (explained below) and to decrease stitches (as shown on the following pages).

MAKE 1 (M1)

This increase is used when increasing stitches after a rib. It is also used for shaping the thumb gusset on gloves and mittens. Use both the right- and left-twisting versions for a neat finish to the gusset. The new stitch is made between two existing stitches using the horizontal thread that lies between the stitches.

To twist M1 to the left

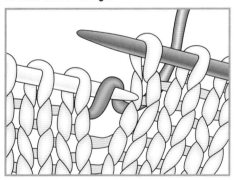

1 Knit to the point where the increase is to be made. Insert the tip of the left-hand needle under the running thread from front to back.

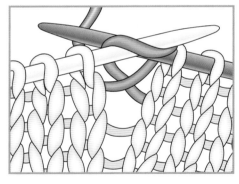

2 Knit this loop through the back to twist it. By twisting it you prevent a hole appearing where the made stitch is.

To twist M1 to the right

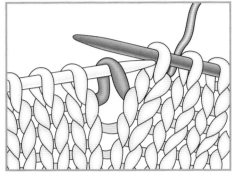

1 Knit to the point where the increase is to be made. Insert the tip of the left-hand needle under the running thread from back to front.

2 Knit this loop through the front to twist it.

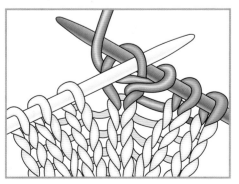

KNIT INTO FRONT AND BACK (KF&B)

This is an easy way to increase one stitch; you work into the front and back of the same stitch. Knit into the front of the stitch as usual. Do not slip the stitch off the left-hand needle, but knit into it again through the back of the loop. Then slip the original stitch off the left-hand needle.

KNIT INTO FRONT, BACK AND FRONT

This increases two stitches instead of one: simply knit into the front, back and then the front again of the same stitch.

(K1, P1, K1) ALL INTO SAME ST

This is also a way of increasing two stitches. Knit into the stitch as normal, do not slip the stitch off the left-hand needle but purl it as normal, and then knit into it again all into the front of the loop.

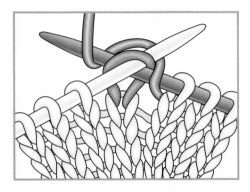

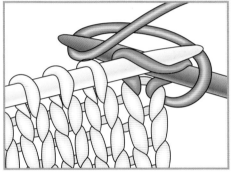

BETWEEN TWO KNIT STITCHES

You can increase one stitch between two knit stitches by (k1, yo, k1) or (k1, yfwd, k1). Bring the yarn forward between the two needles. Knit the next stitch, taking the yarn over the right needle.

AT THE EDGE OF WORK

Sometimes you have to work a yarn over at the edge of the work, before the first stitch. It adds a decorative lacy edge.

Before a knit stitch, bring the yarn forward as if to purl, knit the first stitch bringing the yarn over the right-hand needle as you do so.

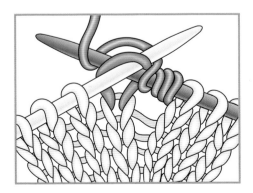

MULTIPLE YARN OVERS
Yo 4 times

Wrap the yarn around the needle four times. On the return row, you must knit into the first loop of the yarn over, purl into the second, knit into the third and purl into the fourth loop.

Yo 5 times

Wrap the yarn around the needle five times. On the return row, work into the first four loops of the yarn over as described for yo 4 times, and then knit into the fifth loop.

decreasing stitches

Decreases are used in many of the projects; they shape the tops of hat crowns to ensure a snug fit. These decreases are also used in the Happy Bunny (see pages 70–73) to form the different sections of the head and body.

DECREASING ONE STITCH

There are a number of ways to decrease one stitch.

K2tog

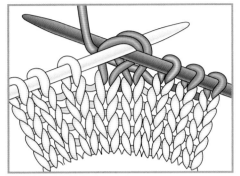

Knit to where the decrease is to be, insert the right-hand needle (as though to knit) through the next two stitches and knit them together as one stitch.

P2tog

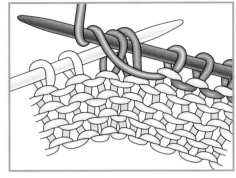

Purl to where the decrease is to be, insert the right-hand needle (as though to purl) through the next two stitches and purl them together as one stitch.

ssk or k2tog tbl

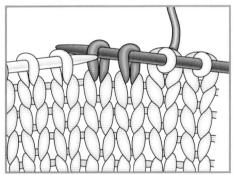

1 Slip two stitches knitwise one at a time from left-hand needle to right-hand needle (they will be twisted).

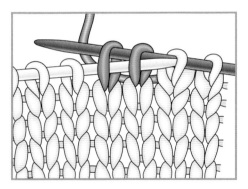

2 Insert the left-hand needle from left to right through the fronts of these two stitches and knit together as one stitch.

ssp or p2tog tbl

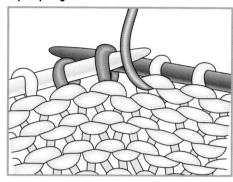 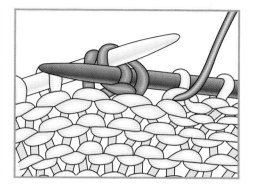

1 Slip two stitches knitwise, one at a time, from the left-hand needle to the right-hand needle (they will be twisted), pass these two stitches back to the left-hand needle in this twisted way.

2 Purl these two stitches together through the back loops.

DECREASING TWO STITCHES AT ONCE

There are various ways of decreasing two stitches at once.

K3tog

Work as k2tog, but knit three stitches together instead of two.

P3tog

Work as p2tog, but purl three stitches together instead of two.

K3tog tbl

Work as ssk (or k2tog tbl), but slip three stitches instead of two and knit them together.

P3tog tbl

Work as ssp, but slip three stitches instead of two and purl them together through the backs of the loops.

sl2tog-k1-psso

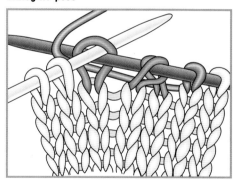 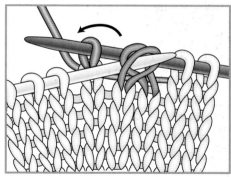

1 Insert the right-hand needle into the next two stitches as if to knit them together, and slip them off together on to the right-hand needle without knitting them. Knit the next stitch.

2 With the tip of the left-hand needle, lift the two slipped stitches together over the knitted stitch and off the needle.

intarsia

Intarsia is a technique of colour knitting, suitable for large blocks of colour or single motifs. Unlike Fair Isle knitting, where the yarn is stranded across the back of the work from one area to another, intarsia uses a separate ball or bobbin of colour for each block. For chunky knit projects, where the yarn is too thick to be wound onto a bobbin, you may need to knit straight from the ball. When you change from one colour to another, you need to twist the yarns together to prevent a hole appearing.

The faces of the Fun Finger Puppets (see pages 74–77) are created using the intarsia method.

BOBBINS

In most cases of intarsia, you don't knit straight from the ball. The exceptions are if the design is very simple, with only two or three colour changes on each row, or if the yarn is thick enough to knit from the ball without becoming too tangled. With each colour change, the yarns are twisted and they will become tangled, making the knitting a chore. If you use bobbins, you can leave them hanging at the back of the work out of the way of other yarns.

You can buy plastic bobbins for intarsia, but it is easy to make your own. Leaving a long end, wind the yarn in a figure of eight around your thumb and little finger. Wind on sufficient to complete the area to be knitted. Cut the yarn and use this cut end to tie a knot around the middle of the bobbin. Use the long end to pull the yarn from the centre of the bobbin.

TWISTING YARNS TOGETHER

The yarns must be twisted to join the blocks of colour together. When you change colour, always pick up the new colour from under the old colour.

WORKING FROM CHARTS

Intarsia patterns are worked from charts. One square represents one stitch and a line of stitches represents one row. The rows are numbered: knit rows (RS rows) are odd numbers and are read from right to left; purl rows (WS rows) are even numbers and are read from left to right. Start knitting from the bottom right-hand corner of the chart at row 1.

TWISTING YARNS ON A PURL ROW

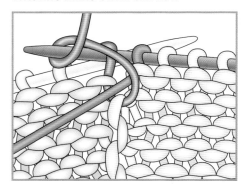

Insert the tip of the right-hand needle into the next stitch, pull the old colour to the left, pick up the new colour and bring it up behind the old colour. Purl the next stitch. The two yarns are twisted together.

TWISTING YARNS ON A KNIT ROW

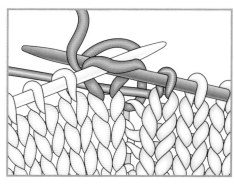

Insert the tip of the right-hand needle into the next stitch, pull the old colour to the left, pick up the new colour and bring it up behind the old colour. Knit the next stitch. The two yarns are twisted together.

WEAVING IN YARN ENDS

Weaving your ends in as you knit is a great time-saving technique. It produces a neat finish when changing colours for stripes or when using multi-yarn balls. In intarsia there will be a lot of ends where colours have begun or ended. You should weave these in as you knit or sew them in every ten rows or so. This removes them from the back where they may become tangled up with the working yarns. It also means that you won't have them to tidy up when you have finished knitting and want to get on with making up the finished project.

Weaving in ends on a knit row

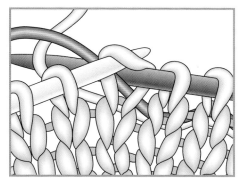

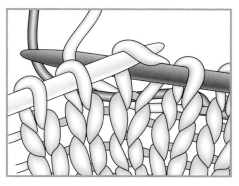

1 Insert the tip of the right-hand needle into the next stitch, bring the cut end over the needle, wrap the yarn around the needle as though to knit.

2 Pull the cut end off the needle and finish knitting the stitch. The cut end is caught into the knitted stitch.

Work the next stitch as normal, then catch the cut end in as before. If you work alternately like this the cut end will lie above and below the row of stitches.

Weaving in ends on a purl row

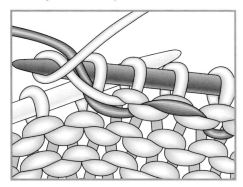

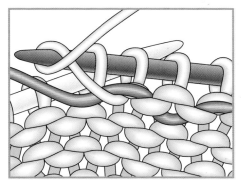

1 Insert the tip of the right-hand needle into the next stitch, bring the cut end over the needle, wrap the yarn around the needle as though to purl.

2 Pull the cut end off the needle and finish purling the stitch. The cut end is caught into the purled stitch.

Work the next stitch as normal, then catch the cut end in as before. If you work alternately like this the cut end will lie above and below the row of stitches.

Small quantities of yarn are used in the pattern around the wrist of these Animal Mittens (see pages 24–29) making them perfect for using up left-over yarns.

SEWING IN ENDS

Where the two colours are twisted together, you will see a line of loops. Using a large-eyed tapestry needle, darn in the end along this line in one direction and then back again for a few stitches.

fair isle knitting

Authentic Fair Isle sweaters were worked as circular knitting so the right side of the knitting was always facing the knitter. This meant that the pattern was always visible and only knit stitches were used.

Today the term Fair Isle knitting is used to describe the technique of knitting with two colours in one row and is used in flat as well as circular knitting.

STRANDING

The loops formed by carrying the yarn between areas of colour are called floats. To get the floats to lie neatly and without lumps where the colours are changed and to prevent the yarns from becoming twisted together and tangled, one colour always lies above the other on the wrong side of the work. By keeping the back of the work neat in this way, the stitches on the front of the work will lie flat without puckering and without holes appearing between the colour changes. Never strand yarns over more than five stitches. In stranding one colour must always be above the other on the back of the work. If they constantly change position, the fabric will be bulky and the yarns will tangle.

WEAVING IN

You must weave the floats in if they are stranded over five stitches or more. This is the same technique used to weave in ends in intarsia (see page 112). Refer to the diagrams and remember to weave the yarn in loosely without pulling up the stitches.

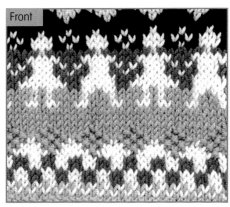

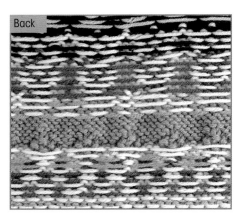

The knitting should be smooth on the front with the yarn floats lying neatly across the back with one colour always above the other.

KNIT PERFECT
There is no need to make bobbins for each colour of yarn. Just use the yarn straight from the ball.

lace knitting

The general term used to cover eyelets, faggoting and lace is lace knitting. These form categories on their own, but many stitch patterns overlap between two or even three of them.

Eyelets are single holes worked in rows or in groups on a background of stockinette stitch that allow a drawstring to be threaded through. Lace is the most open variation where the holes and decreases are arranged to form patterns. A lace stitch pattern can be repeated as an all-over fabric or worked as an insertion on stockinette stitch.

The holes in lace knitting are made by working a yarn over. This makes (increases) a stitch so it has to be accompanied by a decrease. The way you work a yarn over depends on the stitches either side of it. In patterns, where a yarn over (yo) is given, you decide which yarn over method to use. Some patterns will tell you which one to use.

WORKING A YARN OVER

> **KNIT PERFECT**
> A lace pattern needs to be stretched slightly when pressed (see p 119). It needs to be opened out to show off the pattern of the holes. When working a gauge square, pull it out so that it lies flat and the holes are open. Do not every stretch it or it will be distorted.

**Between two knit stitches
(k1, yo, k1) or (k1, yfwd, k1)**

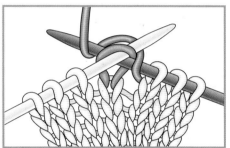

Bring the yarn forward (yfwd or yf) between the two needles. Knit the next stitch, taking the yarn over the right needle.

**Between two purl stitches
(p1, yo, p1) or (p1, yrn, p1)**

Take the yarn back over the right-hand needle and forward between the needles to bring yarn round needle (yrn). Purl the next stitch.

**Between knit and purl stitches
(k1, yo, p1) or (k1, yfrn, p1)**

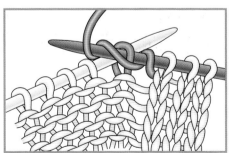

Bring the yarn forward between the two needles, take it back over the right-hand needle and forward again between the two needles – yarn forward and round needle (yfrn). Purl the next stitch.

**Between purl and knit stitches (
p1, yo, k1) or (p1, yon, k1)**

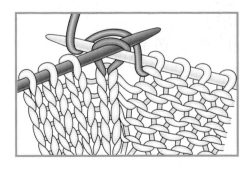

Take the yarn back over the right-hand needle – yarn over needle (yon). Knit the next stitch.

embellishments

Adding embellishments is a lovely way to add a unique and personal finishing touch to your hand-knitted items. We've offered several ideas here for making your own; you could also use shop-bought trims.

POMPOM

Cut two circles out of stiff cardboard. They should be the same diameter that you require for the finished pompom.

Cut out a hole in the centre of each one half of this size. Cut a wedge shape out of the circles. Place them together and begin winding yarn around them until the hole in the centre is filled. Carefully cut through the loops all the way around, being careful not to let any yarn strands escape. Pull a length of yarn between the two pieces of cardboard, knot the two ends together and pull tightly around the centre of the pompom. Secure with a tight knot. Pull out the cardboard circles. Fluff up the pompom, trimming any uneven ends, but leave the two yarn ends for sewing onto your knitted item.

TASSELS

Wrap the yarn loosely around a piece of card the required length of the tassel. Thread a long length of yarn under the strands at the top, fold in half and tie in a tight knot, leaving two long ends. Cut the wrapped strands at the bottom and remove the cardboard. Thread one long end on to a tapestry needle, insert it through the top of the tassel and bring out 1in (2.5cm) below. Wrap the yarn several times around the tassel. Pass the needle through the middle of the wrapped strands to secure the long end, then insert the needle again up through the top of the tassel. Use the long ends to sew in place. Trim the bottom of the tassel neatly.

FRINGE

To make a standard fringe, wrap yarn loosely around a piece of cardboard the required length of the fringe. Cut the wrapped strands at the bottom and remove the cardboard. Fold several lengths in half and, using a crochet or rug hook, pull the strands through the edge of the knitted piece from front to back by catching the fold with the hook. Pass the ends through the folded loop and pull to tighten the knot. Space each bunch of strands evenly along the edge. Trim the bottom of the fringe neatly to the finished length required.

KNOTTED FRINGE

To make a knotted fringe, work as for a normal fringe, with an even number of strands in each bunch. Then take half the strands from one bunch and half the strands from the next one and tie them together. Continue this across the fringe, making sure the knots are in line. The extra knot will take up yarn so make the strands longer than the desired finished length. Try working another row of knots below, combining the original bunches again.

I-CORD

This long tube is knitted on two double-pointed needles; work on needles two sizes smaller than normally used for the yarn.

Cast on 4 stitches onto one of the double-pointed needles and knit one row with the other needle. Do not turn the work but push the stitches to the other end of the needle. Swap the right-hand needle with the left-hand needle, pull the yarn and knit the 4 sts again. Repeat this for every row. By pulling the yarn up at the end of the row, the edges of the knitting are pulled together and the tube is formed. Cast on 3 stitches for a finer cord, and 5 stitches for a thicker one.

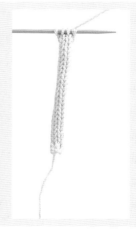

embroidery

Knitted accessories, particularly smaller items such as hats or gloves, can often be enhanced with a little embroidered detail, just to add a further touch of glamour. Some simple embroidery techniques are explained below.

KNIT PERFECT

Use embroidery threads, tapestry wools or knitting yarn; it should be the same or slightly thicker than the knitted yarn. Check that the threads are colourfast and will not shrink when washed. Work an embroidered sample and wash it if you are not certain.

Use a large-eyed blunt tapestry needle. Work the embroidery stitches loosely, don't pull too tightly or the knitted fabric will pucker. To begin the embroidery, weave the end of the thread through a few knitted stitches on the back of the fabric, working back through the thread to secure it; if you start with a knot, it may come undone during wear.

LAZY DAISY STITCH

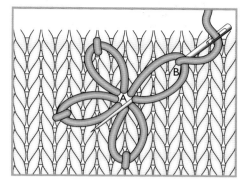

This stitch is formed from individual chain stitches worked around a centre to create the petals of a flower. The loops are fastened with a small stitch. Bring the needle out at A. In one movement, push the needle down in the same place and bring it out at B, looping the thread under the needle tip. Take the needle back down at B, working over the loop, and bring it up at A for the next stitch.

CHAIN STITCH

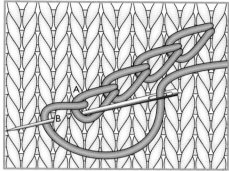

Bring the needle out at A. In one movement, push the needle down in the same place and bring it out at B for the next stitch, looping the thread under the needle tip. To fill the chain stitch, work a straight stitch from the base to the top.

BUTTONHOLE STITCH

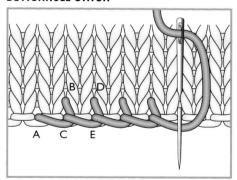

You can use this as a decorative edging along a knitted item, or to reinforce a button loop. Often used to neaten raw edges, this stitch can be worked from left to right or from right to left. Bring the needle out at A. In one movement, take it down at B and back up at C, looping the thread under the needle tip. The next stitch is worked to the right, down at D and up at E. The horizontal threads should lie on the edge of the fabric.

SWISS DARNING

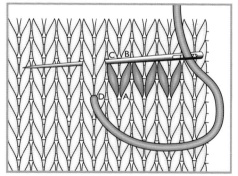

This stitch (also known as duplicate stitch) looks as though it has been knitted into the fabric; it follows the line of the yarn for the knit stitch on the right side of stockinette stitch. It is used to embroider small areas of colour such as a motif that would be tedious to knit, or you can use it to cover up any colours that you don't like in a stripe pattern. Use the same thickness of yarn used for the knitting. Take care to insert the needle between the strands and not to split the knitted stitches. The stitches will appear slightly raised on the surface of the knitting.

Horizontal stitches

Work from right to left, bringing the needle out at the base of the stitch (A). In one movement, take the thread around the top of the stitch by taking the needle down at B and up at C. In one movement, take the needle down at the base of the stitch (A) and up at the base of the next stitch (D). Continue across the row.

Vertical stitches

Work from bottom to top, bringing the needle out at the base of the stitch (A). Take the thread around the top of the stitch (B and C) and back down at the base (A). This time, bring the needle up at the base of the stitch above and continue up the line of knitted stitches.

flowers and leaves

Knitted flowers and leaves are great for embellishing plain garments, such as the Simple Hooded Cardigan (see pages 50–55), to give a feminine touch. Work them in fine, silky yarns for a glamorous look, or crisp cotton yarns that will hold their shape well. If knitted in 100% wool, the fabric can also be fulled. Embellish the edges with beads or embroidery.

SIMPLE KNITTED ROSE

With your chosen yarn and using needles two sizes smaller than those recommended on the ball band, cast on 80 sts and knit 1 row. Work 1in (2.5cm) in st st, beg with a k row.

Dec Row (K2tog) 40 times. 40 sts.
Dec Row (P2tog) 20 times. 20 sts.
Dec Row (K2tog) 10 times. 10 sts.

Cut yarn, leaving a long length. Thread yarn onto a tapestry needle and thread through sts on needle, taking them off the needle one by one. Pull up into gathers. Form the rose by twisting it round and round from the centre with right side of fabric facing outwards. Pull the rose into shape as you go, letting the fabric roll over in some places. Work a few stitches through all layers at the bottom to hold them in place.

For a smaller rose, cast on fewer stitches and work fewer straight rows before decreasing as above.

KNITTED ROSE WITH PETALS
Small [Medium: Large] Petals

(Make 2 of each size)

With your chosen yarn and using needles two sizes smaller than those recommended on the ball band, cast on 3 [3: 4] sts and purl 1 row.

Next Row (Kf&b) 1 [2: 2] times, k2 [1:2]. 4 [5:6] sts.
P 1 row.
Next Row (Kf&b) twice, k2 [3:4]. 6 [7:8] sts.
Work 9 [11:13] rows in st st, starting with a p row.
Next Row (Ssk) twice, k2 [3: 4]. 4 [5:6] sts.
P 1 row.
Next Row (Ssk) 1 [2: 2] times, k2 [1:2].
P1 row.

Bind off, leaving a long end for sewing up. Sew in other end of yarn. Take a small petal, thread the long yarn end onto a large needle and use it to gather the straight edge with a running stitch. Curl the petal around itself with the st st side facing inwards and secure with a few stitches. Gather the second small petal in the same way, curl around the first petal and sew them together at the base. Continue to build up the rose with the two medium and two large petals, overlapping them.

DOUBLE FLOWER
Large Petals (Make 6)

With your chosen yarn and using needles two sizes smaller than those recommended on the ball band, cast on 3 sts and knit 1 row.

Row 1 (RS) K1, (k into front, back and front) into next st, k1. 5 sts.
Rows 2, 4, 6 Knit.
Row 3 K2, (k into front, back and front) into next st, k2. 7 sts.
Row 5 K3, (k into front, back and front) into next st, k3. 9 sts.
Row 7 K4, (k into front, back and front) into next st, k4. 11 sts.
Knit 5 rows.
Row 13 K1, ssk, k5, k2tog, k1. 9 sts.
Knit 5 rows.
Row 19 K1, ssk, k3, k2tog, k1. 7 sts.
Knit 3 rows.
Row 23 K1, ssk, k1, k2tog, k1. 5 sts.
Knit 3 rows.
Row 27 K1, sl2tog, k1, psso, k1. 3 sts.
Knit 1 row.
Row 29 Sl2tog, k1, psso. 1 st.
Cut yarn and thread through rem st.

Small Petals (Make 6)

Cast on 3 sts and knit 1 row.
Work rows 1 to 5 as given for Large Petals. 9 sts.
Knit 5 rows.
Work from row 19 to the end.

To finish...

Fold each petal in half (with RS together) at the base and sew the side edges together for ½in (1.5cm). Place the large petals side by side and run a gathering thread through each to join. Pull the thread tight and repeat through all petals again to form a circle. Pull the thread tight so the flower becomes dish-shaped. Secure the thread. Repeat for the small petals. Sew the inner ring of small petals into the outer ring.

finishing touches

When you have finished knitting all the pieces for your project, you should press them before making up. The knitted pieces will look flatter and you can pull out any side edges so that they are straight. Before pressing, sew in all yarn ends but don't trim them. During pressing, the knitting will stretch and yarn ends can pull through. Wait until the pieces have been pressed.

STEAM PRESSING

This is the method used most for natural yarns such as a pure wool or those with a high wool content. Some yarns with a high synthetic fibre content such as polyester and nylon will not stand the high temperature needed for steaming, so should never be steamed. Always check the ball band before steaming or test on your gauge square first.

Using rustproof pins, pin the knitted piece out, wrong side up, onto an ironing board. If the piece is too big, like some of the larger bags or a long strap, make a pressing board from a folded blanket covered with a sheet. Lay a clean cotton cloth over the pinned-out piece to protect it. Set the steam iron on an appropriate heat setting for the yarn. Hold the iron close to the surface of the knitting without touching it. Do not press the iron on to the knitted fabric. Let the steam penetrate the fabric. Remove the cloth and allow the fabric to dry before unpinning.

WET PRESSING

This is an alternative to steam pressing and is better for synthetics or fancy yarns. Pin out the pieces onto a pressing board, as above. Wet a clean cotton cloth and wring out the excess water until it is just damp. Place it over the pinned-out piece and leave to dry away from direct heat. When the cloth is completely dry, remove it. Make sure the knitted pieces are also dry before you take out the pins and remove them from the board.

SEWING UP

Whenever possible, sew the pieces together with the yarn they are knitted from. If the yarn is something that will break easily or is textured, such as an eyelash yarn or bouclé, use a plain yarn in a matching colour. Do not use the long ends left after knitting the pieces to sew up with; if you do use them and you have to unpick the item for any reason, the ends may start to unravel the knitting. Use a tapestry needle and an 18in (45cm) length of yarn, so the yarn doesn't fray by being passed through the fabric too frequently.

Mattress stitch

To get an invisible seam, use mattress stitch. This is worked from the right side, making it easier to match stripes and shaping details, such as on the sides of bags. Secure the sewing yarn by weaving it down the edge of one of the pieces, bringing it to the front on the first row between the corner and second stitches. Place the two pieces to be joined side by side on a flat surface.

Joining two pieces of stockinette stitch

Having secured the yarn, take the needle across to the opposite side and insert it into the first row between the first and second stitches from front to back, take it under the horizontal strand of the row above and pull the yarn through. Take the needle across to the first edge, insert the needle into the first row between stitches again from front to back, and take it under the horizontal strands of the two rows above. Pull the yarn through. Insert the needle into the opposite edge again, in the same hole that the yarn came out of, and take it under the horizontal strands of the two rows above. Continue zigzagging between the edges, working under two rows each time. Pull the yarn up every few stitches to draw the seam together, but not too tightly – the seam should not pucker the fabric.

Joining two pieces of reverse stockinette stitch

Having secured the yarn, take the needle across to the opposite side and insert it from front to back under the horizontal strand of the row above and pull the yarn through. Take the needle across to the other edge and insert it from front to back under the top loop of the second stitch. Take the needle back to the other edge and work under the strand of the row above. Continue in this way, inserting the needle under the top loop of the second stitch on one edge and under the horizontal strand between the first and second stitches on the other edge. One side of the seam takes in one and a half stitches and the other takes in one stitch, but this weaves the rev st st together so the seam is invisible.

PICKING UP STITCHES

One piece of knitting can be joined to another by picking up stitches and using these instead of casting them on. This eliminates a seam and makes a smoother join.

Hold the work in your left hand with the right side facing. With a needle and the yarn in your right hand, insert the needle under the top of the loop of the first stitch. Wrap the yarn knitwise around the needle and draw through a loop. Continue in this way, inserting the needle under the top loop of each stitch until you have the correct number of stitches.

SEAMS ON THE RIGHT SIDE

Lay the two pieces to be joined together as described in the project instructions. Sew through both thicknesses, one stitch in from the edge, using a small neat running stitch. You can use the knitted fabric as a guide to keep your stitches regular; sew over one stitch and under the next, or over one row and under the next. Do not pull the stitches too tightly or the fabric will pucker.

troubleshooting

Even the most accomplished knitters make mistakes and come up against challenges, so don't be disheartened if you go wrong occasionally. These techniques show you the easy way to rectify your mistakes and find the way forward.

DROPPED STITCHES

A dropped stitch is a stitch that has fallen off your needle and has unravelled down a few rows, creating a ladder. The sooner you spot that you have dropped a stitch, the easier it is to rectify the mistake. Get into the habit of checking your knitting every few rows.

Knit stitch dropped one row below

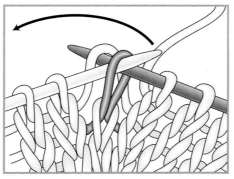

Insert the right needle through the front of the dropped stitch and then pick up the strand of yarn behind it. With the tip of the left needle, pass the stitch over the strand and off the needle.

Purl stitch dropped one row below

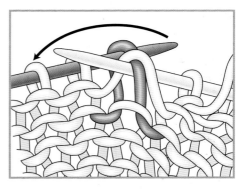

Insert the right needle through the back of the dropped stitch and then pick up the yarn strand in front of it. With the left needle, pass the stitch over the strand and off the needle.

Stitch dropped several rows below

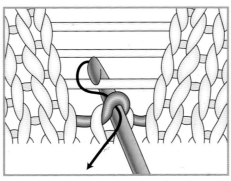

Find the dropped stitch – it will be a loop at the base of a ladder of strands of yarn. Insert a crochet hook through the front of the loop of the dropped stitch, catch the yarn strand immediately above it and pull through the stitch. Repeat for all the strands of the ladder until you reach the top. Slip the stitch back onto the left-hand needle.

To pick up a dropped purl stitch, work as given for a knit stitch but turn your work around so that you are working on the wrong side of the fabric. If more than one stitch has been dropped, slip the others on to a safety pin to stop them running any further, while you pick them up one by one. If you drop a stitch and do not notice it until a lot of knitting later, the ladder will have closed up at the top and there will be no strands of yarn to pick up with the crochet hook. Unfortunately, the only solution is to unravel your work back to the dropped stitch. If you try to pick it up by stealing yarn from the neighbouring stitches, it will create an area of tightened stitches and spoil your knitting.

UNRAVELLING ONE ROW

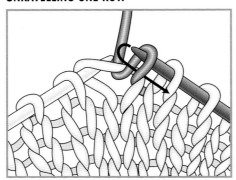

If you have made an error in the stitches that you have just worked on the right needle, for example in a stitch pattern or knitting when you should have purled, there is no need to take the work off the needle to unravel back to that point. You can just unravel, stitch by stitch, back to the error. Insert the left needle into the stitch below from the front, drop the stitch off the right needle and pull the yarn. Repeat this for each stitch back to the error. Work in the same way for purl stitches.

UNRAVELLING SEVERAL ROWS

If you have to unravel several rows, slip the needles out of the stitches carefully, gather the work up into one hand and unravel each row to the row above the error. Do not be tempted to lay the work out flat to do this, as you are more likely to pull the stitches roughly, which often results in you pulling out more than you want. Replace the stitches on to the needle and then unravel the last row carefully as given above. By doing this you have more control over the final row and are less likely to drop or miss any stitches. If you find that after unravelling, your needle is facing the wrong way, slip the stitches purlwise back onto another needle so that you are ready to knit. If you have a suitably sized double-pointed or circular needle, you can use this and then be able to work straight off either end of it.

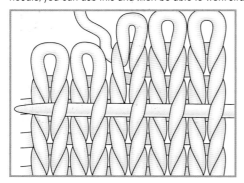

If you are using a slippery yarn or one that will not unravel easily, such as a hairy yarn, or if you are nervous about dropping stitches during unravelling, you can pick up stitches in the row below the error and then unravel knowing the stitches are safe on a needle. Take a spare needle that is smaller than that used for the knitting and weave it through the first loop and over the second loop of each stitch on the row below the mistake. Then pull the work back to these stitches. Make sure you put aside the smaller needle and pick up the correct size to continue knitting.

If you are working a cable or stitch pattern, you should pick the nearest row to the error without too much patterning and where you can see the stitches clearly.

SPLIT YARN

You can easily split a strand of yarn if you are working fast, or, if you are using a yarn mix of several strands, it is easy to miss working through one of the strands. You should go back and rework it correctly, since any split like this will show up on your fabric. Use one of the unravelling methods described to go back to the split stitch.

INCOMPLETE STITCHES

These occur where you have wrapped the yarn around the needle but it has not been pulled through the old stitch to form a new stitch. The yarn strand will be on the needle next to the unworked stitch. Work the stitch properly with the yarn strand as given for dropped stitches.

CABLES

If you have twisted a cable the wrong way, and you have spotted it within a few rows, unravel the cable stitches only and reknit by using the long loops of yarn released by unravelling. If the error is a long way down the piece and the cable has been twisted again after the error, you will have to unravel the work and reknit all of it.

SNAGGED STITCHES

If you snag a stitch, a loop of yarn is pulled out, drawing up tightly several stitches around it. Using a tapestry needle, ease the extra yarn back through the distorted stitches, one by one, starting with the stitch closest to the snag and yarn loop.

RUNNING OUT OF YARN

When you run out of yarn and need to start a new ball or need to change to another colour, always start it at the beginning of a row or at a seam edge where the ends can be woven in neatly.

Simply drop the old yarn, wrap the new yarn around the needle and work a few stitches. Tie the two ends securely together at the beginning of the row so neither one will work its way free and unravel your stitches. When you have finished the piece, undo the knot and weave one end up the edge for a couple of inches, and then double back over a few stitches to secure the end. Make sure you haven't pulled it too tightly and distorted the edge. Weave the other end down the edge using the same method.

If you are coming to the end of a ball, to see if you have enough yarn to work one more row, lay the knitting flat and measure the yarn four times across the width. This will be sufficient to work one row of stockinette stitch; textured and cabled fabric will need more yarn. When in doubt, join in a new ball of yarn to avoid running out of yarn halfway through and having to unravel stitches.

aftercare

Hand-knitted items need to be looked after with some care and love. After you have taken all the effort to make something beautiful, spend time keeping it looking good.

KNIT PERFECT

If in doubt about how your knitted garments will wash, try washing your gauge swatch gently and see how that reacts. If nothing serious happens, then you should be able to hand-wash your knitting carefully.

Hand-dyed yarns, dark colours and some denim yarns contain a lot of excess dye that will wash out. Wash these yarns separately.

KNITTING NOTEBOOK

Keep a ball band from each piece of knitting that you do. Perhaps you could paste it into a notebook, together with a small wrapping of the yarn, as a reminder and also for any mending that may have to be done in the future. The care instructions on the ball band are the best advice to follow when cleaning your knitted items. Instead of writing out long instructions, yarn companies use the same care symbols that are found on garments. Look out for yarns that should be dry cleaned only.

WASHING GARMENTS

Read the care instructions on the ball band; the yarn may be dry-clean only. Before washing, remove any non-washable trims. Usually any trim that you buy will have care instructions with it. The washing information below refers to both natural and synthetic fibres (that are suitable for hand-washing).

For a garment, use cool or lukewarm water and use the same temperature for washing and rinsing, avoiding extremes of temperature. Using a sink or large washing-up bowl, dissolve soap flakes or a special wool-washing solution in lukewarm water. If the soap flakes don't dissolve, add them to hot water, dissolve them and then add plenty of cold water for the right temperature. Lay the knitted item flat and squeeze the soap through the fibres; do not rub or twist the knitting. Take it out of the water, supporting its weight with both hands to stop it stretching. Squeeze out the excess soap and water; do not wring, you will distort the stitches.

RINSING

Refill the sink with clear water of the same temperature as that used for washing. Again, squeeze the water through the knitting; do not pull it out of the water as it is very heavy when waterlogged and will stretch. Rinse it several times, replacing the water each time, until the water runs clear of soap. Take it out of the water, supporting its weight and squeeze out the excess water.

DRYING

Roll the knitting in a colourfast towel to soak up the water. Lay it out flat on a dry towel, pull it back into shape and straighten edges, and leave to dry away from direct heat. If it has any creases or is out of shape when dry, steam press it (see page 119).

If it is a large item, such as a baby blanket, or you are washing several items, you can use the spin cycle on your washing machine to remove excess water. Place the knitting in a pillowcase or duvet cover and tie the end closed. This will stop the knitting being stretched and the stitches catching on anything. Lay the knitting out flat to dry completely. Never use a tumble dryer or hang large heavy pieces on the washing line as they will stretch.

MACHINE WASHING

You should use a delicates or cool wash cycle with a short spin. Place the knitting in a pillowcase or duvet cover, tying the end closed. Remove the knitting as soon as the wash has ended, otherwise it will be badly creased. Lay out flat to dry.

WASHING KNITTED TOYS

When washing knitted toys, hand wash at 30°C and use a detergent suitable for washing delicate fabrics or wool. After you have rinsed the toy, gently squeeze and smooth it out, slightly stretching the knitted fabric in the length in case it has shrunk a little in the wash. You should always wash a toy before giving it to a young child as it will inevitably end up in their mouth!

STORING KNITTING

Store knitting neatly folded in clean, fabric bags to protect them from dust. Fabric bags will allow the knitting to breathe; plastic bags tend to make natural fibres sweat and become damp. Add a moth-repellent, such as moth balls, to wool items. Air the knitting outside before use.

yarns used

Below are listed the specific yarns that were used for the projects in this book, should you wish to recreate them exactly as we have. Yarn companies frequently discontinue colours or yarns, and replace them with new yarns. Therefore, you may find that some of the yarns or colours below are no longer available. However, by referring to the yarn descriptions on the project pages, you should have no trouble finding a substitute.

SUBSTITUTING YARNS

To work out how much replacement yarn you need, follow these simple steps. Use them for each colour or yarn used in the project.
1 The number of balls of the recommended yarn x the number of yards/metres per ball = A
2 The number of yards/metres per ball of the replacement yarn = B
3 A ÷ B = number of balls of replacement yarn.

Page 20 Bootie cuties
Basic shoes
Less than 1 x 1¾oz (50g) ball of Peter Pan Darling DK (100% polyester – 122yd/112m per ball) in shade 365 Powder Blue.
Lilac lovelies
Less than 1 x 1¾oz (50g) ball of Rowan Cashsoft DK (57% extra fine merino wool, 33% microfibre, 10% cashmere – 143yd/131m per ball) in shade 502 Bella Donna.
Blue and white stripes
Less than 1 x 1¾oz (50g) ball of Rowan Calmer (75% cotton 25% acrylic microfibre – 175yd/160m per ball) in shades 160 Drift and 479 Slosh.
Burgundy three-coloured stripes:
Less than 1 x 1¾oz (50g) ball of Rowan Cashsoft DK (57% extra fine merino wool, 33% microfibre, 10% cashmere – 143yd/131m per ball) in shades: **A** 513 Poison, **B** 520 Bloom, **C** 501 Sweet.

Page 24 Animal mittens
Large cheeky chicks mittens
A 1 x 1¾oz (50g) ball of Cygnet Superwash DK (100% wool – 113yd/104m per ball) in shade 298 Cranberry.
Less than 1 x 1¾oz (50g) ball of Cygnet Superwash DK (100% wool – 113yd/104m per ball) in shades **B** 2156 Bluebell, **C** 2817 Everglade and **D** 2155 Gold.
Small sheep mittens
A 1 x 1¾oz (50g) ball of Cygnet Superwash DK (100% wool – 113yd/104m per ball) in shade 2150 Tartan Green.
Less than 1 x 1¾oz (50g) ball of Cygnet Superwash DK (100% wool – 113yd/104m per ball) in shades **B** 2156 Bluebell, **C** 2817 Everglade.
Robin Mittens
A 1 x 1¾oz (50g) ball of Rowan Cashsoft DK (57% extra fine merino, 33% acrylic microfibre, 10% cashmere – 142yd/130m per ball) in shade 520 Bloom.
Less than 1 x 1¾oz (50g) ball of Rowan Cashsoft DK (57% extra fine merino, 33% acrylic microfibre, 10% cashmere – 142yd/130m per ball) in shades **B** 508 Balad Blue and **C** 527 Truffle
D Less than 1 x 1oz (25g) ball of Sidar Snuggly Snowflake double knitting (100% polyester – 92yd/85m per ball) in shade 630 Milky.
Spider Mittens
A 1 x 1¾oz (50g) ball of Rowan Cashsoft DK (57% extra fine merino, 33% acrylic microfibre,

10% cashmere – 142yd/130m per ball) in shade 505 Mist.
Less than 1 x 1¾oz (50g) ball of Sirdar Snuggly DK (55% nylon, 45% acrylic – 191yd/175m per ball) in shades **B** 0377 Putty, **C** 0260 Summer Lime and **D** 312 Black.

Page 30 Lovely lacy set
2 x 1¾oz (50g) balls of Rowan Cashsoft DK (57% extra fine merino, 33% acrylic microfibre, 10% cashmere – 142yd/130m per ball) in shade 500 Cream.
Maroon mittens
Less than 1 x 3½oz (100g) of Rowan Cashsoft DK (57% extra fine merino, 33% acrylic microfibre, 10% cashmere – 142yd/130m per ball) in shade 340 Damson.
Marine mix mittens
Less than 1 x 3½oz (100g) ball of Sirdar Supersoft Aran (100% acrylic – 258yd/236m per ball) in shades 0260 Fern and 0377 Blue.
Baby blue mittens
Less than 1 x 1¾oz (50g) ball of Sirdar Calico DK (60% Cotton, 40% Acrylic – 172yd/158m per ball) in shade 0720 Chambray.

Page 40 Bobbles and stripes set
1 x 1¾oz (50g) ball of Wash 'n' Wear DK Double Crepe (55% acrylic, 45% nylon – 296yd/270m per ball) in shade **A** 236 Scarlet and **B** shade 219 Dusk.
Luscious lilac and taupe
1 x 1¾oz (50g) ball of Rowan Cashsoft DK (57% extra fine merino, 33% acrylic microfibre, 10% cashmere – 142yd/130m per ball) in shades **A** 502 Bella Donna and **B** 515 Tape.
Bold violet and blue
1 x 1¾oz (50g) ball of Cygnet Superwash DK (100% wool – 114yd/104m per ball) in shades **A** 2158 Bluebell and **B** 2185 Geranium.
Spring green and cream
1 x 1¾oz (50g) ball of Cygnet Superwash DK (100% wool – 114yd/104m per ball) in shades **A** 2150 Tartan Green and **B** 2195 Cream.

Page 44 So stripy sweater
2 x 1¾oz (50g) balls of Rowan Cashsoft DK (57% extra fine merino, 33% acrylic microfibre, 10% cashmere – 142yd/130m per ball) in each of shades 500 Cream and 508 Ballad Blue.

Pretty in pink

2 x 1¾oz (50g) balls of Rowan Cashsoft DK (57% extra fine merino, 33% acrylic microfibre, 10% cashmere – 142yd/130m per ball) in shade 520 Bloom.

2 x 1¾oz (50g) balls of Rowan 4 ply Cotton (100% cotton – 186yd/170m per ball) in shade 112 Bleached.

Page 50 Simple hooded cardigan

4 x 1¾oz (50g) balls of Sirdar 'Big Softie' Super Chunky (51% wool, 49% acrylic – 45yd/45m per ball) in shade – 0335 Blancmange.

Sugar and spice

Knit one strand of each of the following yarns together:

2 x 1¾oz (50g) balls of Rowan Cashsoft DK (57% extra fine merino, 33% acrylic microfibre, 10% cashmere –142yd/130m per ball) in each of shade 520 Bloom and 500 Cream.

2 x 1¾oz (50g) balls of Rowan Cashsoft Baby DK (57% extra fine merino, 33% acrylic microfibre, 10% cashmere – 142yd/130m per ball) in shade 807 Pixie.

2 x 1¾oz (50g) balls of Rowan Extra Fine Merino DK (100% merino – 137yd/125m per ball) in shade 892 Mushroom.

Page 56 Pretty pinafore dress

Sirdar Luxury Soft Cotton DK (100% cotton – 104yd/95m per 1¾oz (50g) ball) in shades: **A** 2 balls in 650 Indigo, **B** 1 ball in 661 Pretty Pink, **C** 1 ball in 659 Lilac Blossom.

Festive feel

Cygnet Superwash DK (100% pure wool – 114yd/104m per 1¾oz (50g) ball in shades: **A** 2 balls in 298 Cranberry, **B** 1 ball in 2150 Tartan Green, **C** 1 ball in shade 2156 Bluebell.

Strawberries and cream

Rowan Yarn Cashsoft DK (57% extra fine merino, 33% acrylic microfibre, 10% cashmere yarn – 142yd/130m per 1¾oz (50g) ball) in shades: **A** 2 balls in 801 Horseradish Cream, **B** 1 ball in 520 Bloom, **C** 1 ball in 807 Pixie Pink.

Beautiful blues

Sirdar Snuggly DK (100% polyester – 92yd/85m per 1¾oz (50g) ball) in shades: **A** 2 balls in 377 Putty, **B** 1 ball in 379 Stone, **C** 1 ball in 354 Bluebell

Page 62 Peekaboo pocket cardigan

Cygnet Wool Rich 4ply (75% wool/25% polyamide – 224yd/205m per 1¾oz (50g) ball) in the following shades: **A** 2 balls in 2149 Lilac, **B** 2 balls in 0130 Dove grey, **C** 1 ball in 0268 Olive, **D** 1 ball in 1048 Mauve.

1 x 3½oz (100g) ball of Cygnet DK (100% acrylic –325yd/298m per ball) in shade 146 Mother of Pearl for bear.

Brown bear cardigan

Cygnet Superwash DK (100% wool – 113yd/104m per 1¾oz (50g) ball) in the following shades: **A** 4 x balls in 2156 Bluebell, **B** 1 x ball in shade 2817 Everglade, **C** 1 x ball in shade 2837 Kingfisher.

1 x 3½oz (100g) ball of Cygnet DK (100% acrylic – 325yd/298m per ball) in shade 2297 Chocolate for bear.

Page 70 Happy bunny

1 x 1¾oz (50g) ball of Rowan Cashsoft DK (57% extra fine merino, 33% acrylic microfibre, 10% cashmere –142yd/130m per ball) in shade 505 Mist.

Page 74 Fun finger puppets

Less than 1 x 1¾oz (50g) ball of Rowan Cashsoft DK (57% extra fine merino, 33% acrylic microfibre, 10% cashmere –142yd/130m per ball) in each of the following colours:

Faces: Shade 500 Cream
Friendly lion: Shade 510 Clementine
Cheeky cat: Shade 519 Black
Mischievous monkey: Shade 507 Savannah
Happy hen: Shade 527 Truffle.

Page 78 Cosy toes warmer

5 x 1oz (25g) balls of Sirdar Snuggly Snowflake DK (100% polyester – 92yd/85m per ball) in shade 0631 Creamy.

1 x 1¾oz (50g) ball of Cygnet Truly Wool Rich 4 ply (75% wool, 25% polyamide – 224yd/205m per ball) in shade 2134 Rose Pink.

Autumn tweed

A 2 x 1¾oz (50g) balls of Sirdar Escape DK (51% wool, 49% acrylic – 120yd/110m per ball) in shade 0187 Ecstacy.

B 3 x 1¾oz (50g) balls of Cygnet Wool Rich 4ply (75% wool, 25% nylon – 224yd/205m per ball) in shade 2149 Lilac.

C 1 x 1¾oz (50g) ball of Sirdar Snuggly Baby Bamboo (80% Bamboo, 20% Wool yarn – 104yd/ 95m per ball) in shade 126 Rocking Horse.

Winter blues

A 5 x 1¾oz (50g) balls of Rowan Calmer (75% cotton, 25% acrylic yarn – 175yd/160m per ball) in shade 479 Slosh.

B 1 x 1¾oz (50g) balls of Sirdar 4ply (55% nylon, 45% acrylic yarn – 247yd/226m per ball) in shade 407 Toddle Aqua.

Page 84 Cute chicken mobile

1 x 1¾oz (50g) ball of Rowan Cashsoft DK (57% extra fine merino, 33% acrylic microfibre, 10% cashmere – 142yd/130m per ball) in each of the following shades: **A** 500 Cream, **B** 527 Truffle, **C** 1 x 1¾oz (50g) ball of Rowan Pure Wool DK (100% superwash wool – 137yd/125m per ball) in shade 32 Gilt.

Page 92 Beautiful blanket

5 x 3½oz (100g) balls of Sidar Denim Chunky (60% acrylic, 25% cotton, 15% wool –171yd/156m per ball) in shade 508 Ivory Cream.

Tweed stocking stitch sample

1¾oz (50g) balls of Sirdar Escape DK (51% wool, 49% acrylic – 120yd/110m per ball) in shade 0187 Ecstacy, knitted with 1¾oz (50g) balls of Cygnet Wool Rich 4 ply (75% Wool, 25% Polyamide – 224yd/205m per ball in shade 1048 Mauve.

Pale tweed bramble sample

1¾oz (50g) balls of Cygnet Wool Rich 4 ply (75% Wool, 25% Polyamide – 224yd/205m per ball). Knit strands of each of the following yarns together, as follows: **A** 2 strands of shade 2134 Rose Pink, **B** 1 strand of shade 0130 Dove Grey, **C** 1 strand of shade 131 Baby Blue.

Blue moss stitch sample

14oz (400g) balls of Sirdar Hayfield Bonus Aran (80% Acrylic, 20% Wool – 920yd/840m) per ball in shade 994 Denim Blue.

Page 96 Funky Floral Pyjama bag

1 x 3½oz (100g) balls of Cygnet DK (100% acrylic – 325yd/298m per ball) in the following shades: **A** 377 Emerald, **B** 1255 Saxe, **C** 134 Cerise, Small quantity of **D** 184 Sunshine.

suppliers

Art Yarns
www.artyarns.com
(USA) Art Yarns
39 Westmoreland Avenue,
White Plains, NY 10606
Tel: +1 914 428 0333
(UK) Get Knitted
39 Brislington Hill, Brislington,
Bristol, BS4 5BE
Tel: +44 (0)117 941 2600
www.getknitted.com
(AUS) Mosman Needlecraft Shop 3
529 Military Road, Mosman, NSW 2088
Tel: +61 9969 5105
www.mosmanneedlecraft.com.au
email: mosmanneedlecraft@bigpond.com

Blue Sky Alpacas
(US) Blue Sky Alpacas Inc
PO Box 88, Cedar, MN 55011
Tel: +1 763 753 5815
www.blueskyalpacas.com
email: info@blueskyalpacas.com
(UK) Loop
41 Cross Street, London, N1 2BB
Tel: +44 (0)20 7288 1160
www.loopknitting.com
email: info@loopknitting.com

Colinette
www.colinette.co.uk
(USA) Unique Kolours
28 North Bacton Hill Road,
Malvern, PA, 19355
Tel: +1 800 252 3934
www.uniquekolours.com
email: uniquekolo@aol.com
(UK) Colinette Yarns Ltd
Banwy Workshops,
Llanfair, Caereinion, SY21 0SG
Tel: +44 (0)1938 810128
email: feedback@colinette.com

Crystal Palace Yarns
www.straw.com
(USA) Crystal Palace Yarns
160 23rd Street, Richmond, CA, 94804
(UK) Hantex Ltd
Whitehouse Yard, Eaudyke,
Friskney, Boston, Lincs, PE22 8NL
Tel: +44 (0)1754 820800
www.hantex.co.uk
email: sales@hantex.co.uk

Cygnet Yarns Ltd
(UK) 12–14 Adelaide Street, Bradford, West
Yorkshire, BD5 0EF
Tel:+44 1274 743374
web: www.cygnetyarns.com
email: sales@cygnetyarns.com

Debbie Bliss
www.debbieblissonline.com
(USA) Knitting Fever Inc.
315 Bayview Avenue, Amityville,
NY, 11701
Tel: +1 516 546 3600
www.knittingfever.com
email: admin@knittingfever.com
(UK) Designer Yarns Ltd
Units 8–10 Newbridge Industrial Estate
Pitt Street, Keighley,
West Yorkshire, BD21 4PQ
Tel: +44 (0)1535 664222
www.designeryarns.co.uk.com
email: enquiries@designeryarns.uk.com
(AUS) Prestige Yarns Pty Ltd
PO Box 39, Bulli, NSW 2516
Tel: +61 (0)2 4285 6669
www.prestigeyarns.com
email: info@prestigeyarns.com

DMC
(USA) The DMC Corporation
77 South Hackensack Avenue, Bldg 10F,
South Kearney, NJ 07032-4688
Tel: +1 973 589 0606
www.dmc-usa.com
(UK) DMC Creative World Ltd
Pullman Road, Wigston, Leicester LE18 2DY
Tel: +44 (0)116 281 1040
www.dmc.com
(AUS) See website for stockists

GGH
(USA) My Muench Yarns Inc
1323 Scott Street, Petaluma, CA, 94954-1135
Tel: +1 (707) 763 9377
e-mail: info@muenchyarns.com
www.muenchyarns.com
(UK) Loop
41 Cross Street, London, N1 2BB
Tel: +44 (0)20 7288 1160
e-mail: info@loop.gb.com
www.loopknittingshop.com

Jo Sharp
www.josharp.com.au
(USA) JCA Inc.
35 Scales Lane, Townsend, MA 01469
www.jcacrafts.com
Tel: +1 978 597 8794
(AUS) Jo Sharp Hand Knitting Yarns
PO Box 357, Albany, WA, 6331
Tel: +61 (0)8 9405 8207
email: yarn@josharp.com.au

Kaalund
www.kaalundyarns.com.au
(USA) Jumbuck Fibers
San Juan, Capistrano, California
Tel: +1 949 481 6696
Email: jumbuk1@me.com
(UK) Kangaroo
Knights Court, Bevernbridge
South Chailey, BN8 4QF
Tel: +44 (0)1273 400030
www.kangaroo.uk.com
(AUS)Kaalund Yarns Pty Ltd
PO Box 17, Banyo, Qld 4014
Tel: +61 (0)7 3267 6266
email: yarns@kaalundyarns.com.au

Louisa Harding
www.louisaharding.co.uk
(USA) EuroYarns
315 Bayview Avenue, Amityville, NY, 11701
Tel: +1 516 546 3600
www.euroyarns.com
(UK) Designer Yarns Ltd
Units 8–10 Newbridge Industrial Estate,
Pitt Street, Keighley, West Yorkshire, BD21 4PQ
Tel: +44 (0)1535 664222
www.designeryarns.co.uk.com
email: enquiries@designeryarns.uk.com
(AUS) Prestige Yarns Pty Ltd
PO Box 39, Bulli, NSW 2516
Tel: +61 (0)2 4285 6669
www.prestigeyarns.com
email: info@prestigeyarns.com

Noro
www.eisakunoro.com
(USA) Knitting Fever Inc.
315 Bayview Avenue
Amityville, NY 11701
Tel: +1 516 546 3600
www.knittingfever.com

(UK) Designer Yarns Ltd
Units 8–10 Newbridge Industrial Estate,
Pitt Street, Keighley, West Yorkshire,
BD21 4PQ
Tel: +44 (0)1535 664222
www.designeryarns.co.uk.com
email: enquiries@designeryarns.uk.com
(AUS) Prestige Yarns Pty Ltd
PO Box 39, Bulli, NSW 2516
Tel: +61 (0)2 4285 6669
www.prestigeyarns.com
email: info@prestigeyarns.com

Patons
www.coatscrafts.co.uk
(USA/CAN) 320 Livingstone Avenue South,
Listowel, ON, Canada, N4W 3H3
Tel: +1 888 368 8401
www.patonsyarns.com
email: inquire@patonsyarns.com
(UK) Coats Crafts UK
PO Box 22, Lingfield House, Lingfield Point,
McMullen Road, Darlington DL1 1YJ
Tel: +44 (0)1325 394237
www.coatscrafts.co.uk
email: consumer.ccuk@coats.com
(AUS) Patons
PO Box 7276, Melbourne, Victoria 3004
Tel: +61 (0)3 9380 3888
www.patons.biz
email: enquiries@auspinners.com.au

Peter Pan
(UK) Thomas B. Ramsden & Co
Netherfield Road, Guiseley, Leeds, LS20 9PD
Tel: +44 1943) 872264
www.tbramsden.co.uk
email: enquiries@tbramsden.co.uk

Rowan
www.knitrowan.com
(USA) Westminster Fibers Inc
165 Ledge Street, Nashua, New Hampshire, 03060
Tel: +1 603 886 5041/5043
www.westminsterfibers.com
email: info@westminsterfibers.com
(UK) Rowan
Green Lane Mill, Holmfirth HD9 2DX
Tel: +44 (0)1484 681881
email: info@knitrowan.com

(AUS) Australian Country Spinners Pty Ltd
Level 7, 409 St. Kilda Road
Melbourne, Victoria, 3004
Tel: +61 (0)3 9380 3888
email: tkohut@auspinners.com.au

Sirdar
www.sirdar.co.uk
(USA) Knitting Fever Inc.
315 Bayview Avenue, Amityville, NY, 11701
Tel: +1 516 546 3600
www.knittingfever.com
(UK) Sirdar Spinning Ltd
Flanshaw Lane, Alvethorpe, Wakefield, WF2 9ND
Tel: +44 (0)1924 371501
email: enquiries@sirdar.co.uk
(AUS) Creative Images
PO Box 106, Hastings, Victoria 3915
Tel: +61 (0)3 5979 1555
email: creative@peninsula.starway.net.au

South West Trading Company
www.soysilk.com
(USA) See website for stockists
(UK) Create & Knit
The Old Granary Studios, Priory Nurseries,
Breedon on the Hill, Derbyshire, DE73 8AT
Tel: +44 (0)7594 437948
www.createandknit.co.uk
(AUS) See website for stockists

Sublime
www.sublimeyarns.com
(USA) Knitting Fever Inc
PO Box 336, 315 Bayview Avenue
Amityville, NY, 11701
Tel: +1 516 546 3600
www.knittingfever.com
admin@knittingfever.com
(UK) Sublime Yarns
Flanshaw Lane, Wakefield, West Yorkshire,
WF2 9ND
Tel: +44 (0)1924 369666
email: contactus@sublimeyarns.com
(AUS) Creative Images
PO Box 106, Hastings, Victoria 3915
Tel:+61 (0)3 5979 1555
email: creative@peninsula.starway.net.au

Twilleys
www.twilleys.co.uk
(UK) Twilleys of Stamford
Roman Mill, Stamford PE9 1BG
Tel: +44 (0)1780 752661
email: twilleys@tbramsden.co.uk

about the author

Laura Long graduated in 2003 with a first class honours degree in Knitted Textiles from Central St Martins College of Art and Design. Since then she has been working out of her Central London studio creating knitted products that are sold in boutiques and galleries all over the world. She has created pieces and written patterns for numerous companies including John Rocha, Rowan yarns and *Knit Today*, *Yarn Forward* and *Simply Knitting* magazines. She is the author of *Knitted Toy Tales* published by D&C in 2009.

acknowledgments

Thank you to everyone and David and Charles, particularly Jennifer Fox-Proverbs for commissioning the book, Sarah Clark for her beautiful design work, James Brooks for his project management skills, and Lorraine Slipper and Bethany Dymond for editing the text. Thank you also to Lorna Yabsley and Sam Atkinson for taking such beautiful photographs and most importantly to my mum for helping to knit all the pieces.

index